Holding

GOD'S HAND

Two-Minute Meditations
for Everyday Challenges

EDITORS OF GUIDEPOSTS

Guideposts
New York

Holding God's Hand

Published by Guideposts Books & Inspirational Media
110 William Street
New York, New York 10038
Guideposts.org

Acknowledgments

Every attempt has been made to credit the sources of copyrighted material used in this book. If any such acknowledgment has been inadvertently omitted or miscredited, receipt of such information would be appreciated.

Scripture quotations marked (AMP) are from the *Amplified Bible*. Copyright © 1954, 1958, 1962, 1964, 1965, 1987 by the Lockman Foundation.

Scripture quotations marked (ESV) are taken from the *Holy Bible, English Standard Version*, copyright © 2001 by Crossway Bibles, a division of Good News Publishers. Used by permission. All rights reserved.

Scripture quotations marked (KJV) are taken from The King James Version of the Bible.

Scripture quotations marked (MSG) are taken from *The Message*. Copyright © 1993, 1994, 1995, 1996, 2000, 2001, 2002 by Eugene H. Peterson.

Scripture quotations marked (NAS) are taken from the *New American Standard Bible*, copyright © 1960, 1962, 1963, 1968, 1971, 1972, 1973, 1975, 1977, 1995 by the Lockman Foundation. Used by permission.

Scripture quotations marked (NIV) are taken from *The Holy Bible, New International Version*. Copyright © 1973, 1978, 1984, 2011 by Biblica, Inc. Used by permission of Zondervan. All rights reserved worldwide. www.zondervan.com

Scripture quotations marked (NKJV) are taken from *The Holy Bible, New King James Version*. Copyright © 1982 by Thomas Nelson, Inc.

Scripture quotations marked (NLT) are from the *Holy Bible, New Living Translation*. Copyright © 1996, 2004, 2007 by Tyndale House Foundation. Used by permission of Tyndale House Publishers Inc., Carol Stream, Illinois 60188. All rights reserved.

Scripture quotations marked (NRSV) are taken from the *New Revised Standard Version Bible*. Copyright © 1989 by the Division of Christian Education of the National Council of the Churches of Christ in the United States of America. Used by permission. All rights reserved.

Scripture quotations marked (RSV) are taken from the *Revised Standard Version of the Bible*. Copyright © 1946, 1952, 1971 by Division of Christian Education of the National Council of Churches of Christ in the United States of America. Used by permission.

Scripture quotations marked (TLB) are taken from *The Living Bible*. Copyright © 1971 by Tyndale House Publishers, Wheaton, Illinois 60187. All rights reserved.

Scripture quotations marked (TNIV) are taken from *Holy Bible, Today's New International Version* Copyright © 2001, 2005 by Biblica. All rights reserved worldwide.

Cover and interior design by Müllerhaus
Cover photo/art by Shutterstock
Typeset by Aptara
Index by Indexing Research

Printed and bound in the United States of America
10 9 8 7 6 5 4 3 2

Contents

Introduction

WE ALL HAVE DAYS WHEN NOTHING SEEMS TO BE GOING RIGHT AND THE stresses and strains of life are trying our patience and frazzling our spirits. It's in those moments that we need to pause and take a moment to rejuvenate and refresh our souls in the presence of God.

Holding God's Hand is designed to do just that—to give your spirit a quick pick-me-up. It's organized into nine point-of-need chapters, including When You Need Healing, When You Feel Anxious, and When You Feel Lonely. Each is filled with powerful two-minute meditations, plus spiritual quotes, Bible verses, prayers, and spiritual direction that guide your thoughts toward a serene and tranquil place of rest—a place full of God's peaceful presence. Think of it as your one-stop spiritual first-aid kit that you will be relieved to have on hand for those moments when life challenges your patience, courage, resolve, and faith. From facing the loss of a loved one, going through financial struggles, or battling illness, to the challenges of caregiving, loneliness, or grief, these powerful personal stories of perseverance, coupled with practical suggestions for moving on, will quiet your mind, restore your soul, and place you back in the light and care of God.

As you read the opening Scriptures, reflect on the spiritually nourishing vignettes, pray along with the writers, and follow the guiding steps they provide, you'll find that these one-page meditations will help you find peace of mind, whether it's in your morning or evening prayer time or in the tougher moments of any day. At your bedside, on your desk, or in your workplace, it is our prayer that *Holding God's Hand* will help you turn your everyday hassles into moments of grace, giving you a renewed mind and a hope-filled spirit.

It's the perfect companion to keep within reach for your trying moments or to share with others in need.

Whether you turn to a chapter that reflects your mood, or use the index to take you directly to a situation just like the one you are facing, *Holding God's Hand* is like having a soothing cup of tea on a sunlit morning. In just a few minutes, you'll be refreshed!

And if you have a concern that you would like us to pray for, please contact OurPrayer, Guideposts' prayer ministry that lifts our challenges and joys to God. You can submit prayer requests by visiting OurPrayer.org and Facebook .com/OurPrayer or writing to us at OurPrayer, PO Box 5813, Harlan, Iowa 51593–1313.

Editors of Guideposts

*For I am the Lord your God who takes hold of your right hand and
says to you, Do not fear; I will help you.*
—Isaiah 41:13 (NIV)

Chapter 1

WHEN YOU NEED HEALING

....

Crisis brings us face to face with our inadequacy and our inadequacy in turn leads us to the inexhaustible sufficiency of God.

CATHERINE MARSHALL

HEART-CHANGING PRAYERS

Be joyful in hope, patient in affliction, faithful in prayer. —ROMANS 12:12 (NIV)

SPRING, A TIME OF REBIRTH, ARRIVED EARLY FOR ME THIS YEAR. ON MARCH 16, my wife drove me to the hospital because I just didn't feel right. "It's not cardiac," I assured each doctor and nurse who examined me, hooked me up to a monitor, or drew blood. The heart specialist wanted me to undergo a stress test and echocardiogram. "It's not cardiac," I told him, but he tested me anyway. "It's cardiac," I said to my wife after I was placed on the gurney, given a nitro, and wheeled into the cath lab.

I have been comforted by prayers before but never in emergency situations. Family, friends, and church members prayed when I had a mole removed, when a test revealed that I had melanoma, and when a biopsy indicated the cancer had not spread. Those prayers helped me to be "patient in affliction."

There is no time to be patient during a cardiac emergency. But when my wife informed me, just before a stent was being placed in a blocked coronary artery, that my family and friends were praying, I felt comfort such as I had never felt before.

Later that week, when the first day of spring actually arrived, I puzzled over the power of prayer. I will never know if the prayers on my behalf changed the outcome of the operation on my heart. I have learned that when people pray for us, the awareness of their prayers is positively heart-changing. —TIM WILLIAMS

Dear God, thank You for the faithful people who surround us
with prayers when we need them.

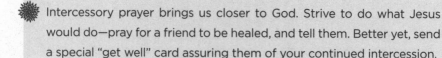 Intercessory prayer brings us closer to God. Strive to do what Jesus would do—pray for a friend to be healed, and tell them. Better yet, send a special "get well" card assuring them of your continued intercession.

GOD ALWAYS ANSWERS

"When I shut up the heavens so that there is no rain…if my people…will humble themselves and pray…then I will hear from heaven…and will heal their land."
—2 Chronicles 7:13–14 (NIV)

The Scripture above was printed in the bulletin at the National Day of Prayer service I attended. *This is such a powerful promise*, I thought. *But sometimes when I'm praying, I'm not sure anything is really improving.*

The next morning when I ventured out on my prayer walk, it was misting ever so slightly, so I took an umbrella just in case. We were in the middle of a severe drought, and the grass was brown and burned up in the highway medians. Things had been dry for so long that I didn't want to get my hopes up. *Just like I feel when I'm praying*, I thought wearily.

An hour later as I neared home, I was surprised when big raindrops began to hit my face. I quickly opened the umbrella. Suddenly, I was walking through a downpour. I stopped and watched a fast-moving stream of rainwater cascading down the curb to the bottom of the hill, carrying with it dust, pollen, and dead leaves. I took a deep breath, drinking in the beautiful smell of the newly cleansed earth. As my feet made a satisfying splash along the sidewalk in rhythm with the rain beating against my umbrella, I remembered the promise from 2 Chronicles: *If my people…will humble themselves and pray…then I…will heal their land.*

I smiled. God hears. God is always answering. So don't ever forget your umbrella when you pray for an outpouring. —Karen Barber

Dear Father, thank You for reassuring us that when we offer our prayers as a country You hear and answer. Amen.

Imagine yourself walking in the rain under God's big umbrella. Recognize how His wonderfully specific blessings are pouring down on you.

SEEING PAST THE PAIN

The human spirit can endure in sickness.... —PROVERBS 18:14 (NIV)

"ERIKA, THIS HAS BEEN YOUR HOME FOR NINETEEN YEARS," BRUCE, THE ranch owner, told me. "You can stay here as long as you want, even if you never heal. But we can't afford to keep your cattle. They have to be sold."

I'd ruptured a disc in my back while fighting a fire on the ranch, and now my greatest fear, losing my ability to ranch, was being realized. But as I stood on the slippery slope of depression, I saw that God had sent comfort.

Within a week of my injury, my friend Lori flew in to Oregon from Georgia and got me through the first series of tests. She called daily to see that I was okay. She believed in me, even when I didn't believe in myself.

My boyfriend, Randy, was by my side too. I was limping through the hospital lobby when another patient eyed me with pity. Randy told him excitedly, "It's a miracle! She was in a wheelchair!" That triggered helpless laughter, and for that moment pain lost its power.

Healing happens when I can make myself see past the pain. It's hard to do, but when mocked, pain weakens. Not a lot, but enough that it's noticeable. I was able to continue on because of my family and friends. They looked after me, supported me.

I know how much I've lost, but I've started to see what I've gained. Leaning on others isn't about my weakness. It's about God's strength. —ERIKA BENTSEN

Lord, whenever I think You've forgotten me,
You send encouragement from friends and strangers.
These daily miracles are proof that You are with me always.

✳ The Bible says God's strength is made perfect in weakness. Thank God for a time when this biblical concept was proven true for you.

SLOWLY AT WORK

He healeth the broken in heart, and bindeth up their wounds. —PSALM 147:3 (KJV)

I REALIZED THIS WEEK THAT I'M A BROKEN PERSON CARRYING THE SCARS of childhood traumas. At work, a man's suggestive comments and aggressive behavior had become so disturbing that I'd grown afraid. When he followed me outdoors one night with even more to say, I went a little crazy. "Get away from me!" I screamed over and over, my throat hurting. "Get away from me! GET AWAY FROM ME!" He switched to derision, and what followed was a regular hullabaloo when my boss came out, alerted by all the hollering.

The ruckus left me badly shaken. *What's the matter with me?* I wondered. *I thought I was a bigger person than this. And doesn't God expect better of me?*

I thought of my granddaughter. Last month, two-year-old Evelyn broke her leg. When her dad called to tell me, the news made me sick to my stomach. The next day when she arrived at my house, asleep in her car seat, curls spilling down over her face, I nearly cried. Life is so fragile. We break so easily.

Today, Evelyn is limping about in her cast, God's healing process slowly at work. None of us expect more of her than she's capable of. We carry her when she can't manage. Isn't this what God does for us? For me? Doesn't He feel "sick to His stomach" when we break, when our psyches and souls suffer pain? —BRENDA WILBEE

Dear God, help me to trust Your healing process,
slow as it may seem, knowing that You don't expect more of me than
I'm capable of and that You carry me when I can't manage on my own.

Today, seek God's healing mercies in addition to treatment for what ails you.

THE HEALING POWER OF PETS

Heal me, O Lord, and I shall be healed; save me, and I shall be saved....
—JEREMIAH 17:14 (AMP)

A FRIEND TOLD ME THAT THE PURRING OF CATS HAS A HEALING POWER. I wasn't so sure. Perhaps it's because our cat, a large Maine coon mix that was rescued from the subway platform, is a less-than-perfect pet. Fred won't sit in my lap for more than thirty seconds and never voluntarily. He likes to wake us up at 6:00 AM for his breakfast, even when there's food still in the bowl. He claws at the sofa. He unloads cat hair in remarkable quantities (you could knit a sweater from the stuff we collect). Fortunately, he's good at purring.

Take out his brush, he purrs. Sit next to him on the bed, he purrs. Scratch him on the flat part of his nose, he purrs so loud I think the neighbors can hear. That his purring can be healing was revealed to me the other night.

It was 3:00 AM, and I wasn't sleeping well. Too many things were going through my mind. I was doing my best to pray through the worries—give them back to God—without much success.

Then Fred leaped up on the bed and meowed. "No, Fred," I whispered, "it's not time for breakfast." He lay down next to my head, his tail twitching, and purred, an incredibly loud, comforting, satisfying sound. It turned out to be just what I needed. I scratched him on the forehead and I'm not sure where the worries went, but the next time I woke up it was 6:10 AM. Fred was letting me know he was hungry.

"Thanks for the extra ten minutes, pal," I told him. And for the purring.
—RICK HAMLIN

God, You have so many ways of giving me Your healing touch.

✺ Use your Bible concordance to search out Scriptures on God's healing.

THANK GOD FOR DAILY RECOVERY

But without faith it is impossible to please him: for he that cometh to God must believe that he is, and that he is a rewarder of them that diligently seek him.
—HEBREWS 11:6 (KJV)

IT'S BEEN MORE THAN TEN YEARS SINCE I WAS LAST TREATED FOR CANCER—the non-Hodgkin's lymphoma variety—third grade, fourth stage, they told me. The third regimen of chemo, in combination with stem cells drawn from my own good bone marrow, achieved a remission. Though many succumb to the disease, the Lord apparently had more work for me to do. The chemo scarred my lungs and made it more difficult to breathe, but I thank God daily for my recovery.

At one stage I considered throwing in the towel, but my oncologist challenged me with a maxim I'll never forget. "You can stop here, if you choose, but to catch the brass ring you'll need to get on the merry-go-round."

For a moment I was puzzled. Then I remembered riding on the carousel: To get a free ride, you had to catch the brass ring as you whirled around. I prayed about the decision and was led to go on. —FRED BAUER

When trouble like thunder shatters our soul, we know that You,
Lord, can make the broken whole.

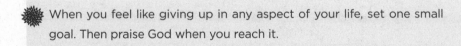 When you feel like giving up in any aspect of your life, set one small goal. Then praise God when you reach it.

SHARING IN THE HEALING PROCESS

Jesus wept. Then said the Jews, Behold how he loved him!
—JOHN 11:35–36 (KJV)

"HOW ARE YOU?" CONCERNED FRIENDS ASKED WHEN THEY LEARNED OF MY depression. Why was that question so hard to answer? A small book by minister Barbara Crafton helped me to understand. She had suffered from clinical depression, and being in the ministry had magnified all the hesitations and pain of being deeply depressed.

The title of her book, *Jesus Wept: When Faith and Depression Meet*, refers to the only time in the Bible when Jesus weeps. When His friend Lazarus, died.

Like us, Christ felt grief and mental anguish and clearly made no effort to hide His sadness. We are often less willing to reveal our pain and vulnerability. I know, because I hid my pain for long enough to make it more serious. I was ashamed that I couldn't "snap out of it." *If my relationship with God is strong, why am I feeling so hopeless?* I wondered. *If I pray hard enough, why doesn't God lighten the darkness?* I felt as if people saw me as missing spiritual strength.

But quiet words from someone who understands can break through the bleak isolation. I've read Crafton's book four or five times. Her healing became a part of mine. Now back on solid ground, I can repeat to myself her words: "We are children of God, put here to delight in the world as long as we are privileged to be here." —BRIGITTE WEEKS

Lord, I need Your care on the good days and the bad,
and I trust that You will never leave me alone in the dark. Amen.

Select a pretty jar and place it on your nightstand to remind you of God's promise to collect all of your tears in a bottle (Psalm 56:8).

GOD CAN HEAL IT ALL

Lord, you alone can heal me, you alone can save, and my praises are for you alone.
—JEREMIAH 17:14 (TLB)

A NUMBER OF MY CLOSE FRIENDS AND FAMILY MEMBERS WERE EXPERIENCING lost jobs, marriages on the brink, homes going into foreclosure. My heart ached because I could not solve their problems.

Then I had hand surgery that left a five-inch wound in the shape of a Y on my left palm. As I went through occupational therapy to get the feeling back in my hand and fingers, I was absolutely amazed at how my body healed itself. Each day I could see a noticeable improvement from the day before. After day eleven when the stitches came out, my hand seemed to heal even faster.

I thought about my loved ones' problems as I watched my hand heal. I learned what an absolutely perfect engineer God is. If God could create a body that heals itself, there was no doubt that God could heal the problems of my friends and family who were hurting. At that moment, my heart started to heal, knowing they were in the hands of a creative genius. All it took to get things started was prayer and faith. —PATRICIA LORENZ

> *Master of all creation, how brilliant You are for giving me*
> *the ability to grow new skin, heal my wounds, regenerate my*
> *body, and solve life's problems over and over and over again.*

 Do you have a scar? Look at it today and reflect on what God brought you through.

WHEN TWO ARE GATHERED IN HIS NAME

Now there are varieties of gifts, but the same Spirit; and there are varieties of service, but the same Lord. —1 CORINTHIANS 12:4–5 (RSV)

THAT SUNDAY MORNING, I COULD HAVE USED SOME HEALING. FOR WEEKS I'd been fighting an infection. I wasn't terribly sick, but I was weary of trips to the doctor's office with no specific answer. That day, sitting in the choir loft during worship, I looked over and saw my friend Roberta.

Roberta is a healer. She's an RN with an advanced degree. Yet she also has spiritual gifts, and I've known her to pray for people who need healing. It seemed a lot to ask, and I didn't quite know how to bring it up.

The choir room was clearing out at the end of the service. "Roberta," I said, "I've had this infection for a while…"

"Shall I pray for you?" she asked.

We found a quiet corner in the back of the hall and talked. Then we closed our eyes, and she prayed for my healing. I prayed too—for myself and for Roberta—that her daughter would find her way in life.

"Amen," she said. I opened my eyes. I didn't know about the mysterious infection, but I certainly felt better. A little more hopeful that it would finally go away.

"I hope you feel better," I told her.

"I always do," she said. "That's one of the things that comes with healing. I get more back than I could possibly give."

I had been hesitant to ask, but what a gift she had shared. —RICK HAMLIN

Lord, may I never be too timid to share my gifts or
ask people to share theirs.

If you don't already have a prayer partner, seek one out today. If you do, ask them to pray with you about whatever is on your heart.

THE LORD'S COMFORT

Present yourselves to God as those who have been brought from death to life, and
present your members to God as instruments of righteousness.
—ROMANS 6:13 (NRSV)

I LIKE TO PRAY IN DIFFERENT WAYS AND IN UNUSUAL PLACES. SOMETIMES I try to incorporate movement and imagination into my prayers.

So when I feel helpless, confused, or in need of comfort, I envision the Lord cradling me as He would cradle an infant. If I'm praying for my marriage, I picture Him walking with Charlie and me, arm in arm, or holding our hands as we all walk together. When I pray for someone who's ill, I imagine the Lord holding that person or raining a healing light down upon him or her. And when I pray for healing or forgiveness for myself, I throw my arms up into the air and ask Him to pour out His forgiveness and healing on me.

I was praying this way recently when it occurred to me that I might have it all backward. I'd opened my arms to the Lord, praying that He would pour His forgiveness and healing over me, but wasn't I missing a step? Shouldn't I be opening my arms to the Lord first to acknowledge and release the sin and the sickness I needed Him to forgive and heal? Only after I'd willingly relinquished these maladies of the soul and body to God, trusting that He would remove them, could I sincerely ask for the forgiveness and healing I sought.
—MARCI ALBORGHETTI

Jesus, You know my flaws and frailties. As I pray in Your name,
give me the courage to trust them to Your healing Spirit.

Find a spot in nature that has special meaning for you. Open your arms to Jesus there, and ask Him to touch your body, mind, and spirit with His healing balm.

HE PRAYED FOR THE SICK

And Jesus went forth, and saw a great multitude, and was moved with compassion toward them, and he healed their sick. —MATTHEW 14:14 (KJV)

I WAS SITTING IN THE CROWDED WAITING ROOM OF ST. THOMAS HOSPITAL. I was with my son Jon, who was having some tests done. He needed me to drive him. I'd buried myself in a newspaper article on pet-sitting. The room was hot; the intercom was noisy; someone was coughing; a child was crying. I buried myself deeper in the paper.

"Patient forty-two," called the intercom once, then twice.

A nurse came out to look for her patient. "Is number forty-two here?"

He was sitting alone, next to me, emaciated, in torn blue jeans and a faded flannel shirt. "I'm sorry," he said nervously. "I didn't hear."

I watched him over the edge of my paper, shuffling behind the nurse. I put down my paper and looked around, noticing—really noticing—my surroundings. There was a chunky, pasty-skinned woman clutching a walker. There was an elderly woman in a wheelchair, assisted by a stooped, frail-looking man. In the corner, a tired-looking woman held a small, fussy child.

As my eyes roamed, I saw a crucifix on the wall. From across the crowded room, I could feel Jesus looking at me with compassion and pleading, reminding me that even on the Cross He was present to the pain and suffering of those around Him. He took care of His mother, He prayed for His enemies, and He healed the soul of the thief crucified next to Him.

What do You want, Lord? I asked. But I already knew. —SHARI SMYTH

Jesus, forgive me for my indifference. I pray for these,
Your suffering ones. Bring healing and peace to them.

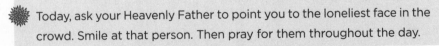 Today, ask your Heavenly Father to point you to the loneliest face in the crowd. Smile at that person. Then pray for them throughout the day.

HEALING POWER OF HYMNS

*I will wait for the God of my salvation.... —*MICAH 7:7 (NAS)

IN MY HOSPITAL ROOM, I WAS VISITED BY A DOCTOR WEARING A GOWN AND mask. This new lung specialist explained that he didn't think I had a blood clot in my lungs. Rather, he thought I might have tuberculosis.

When I was a brand-new registered nurse in 1974, I had performed mouth-to-mouth resuscitation on a lady who was later found to have active pulmonary tuberculosis. I'd had a positive TB skin test, and the doctor feared that I had reactivated that old infection. I was now to be in isolation for three days until they could test my sputum for *Mycobacterium tuberculosis.*

The irony of the situation wasn't lost on me. I was an infection-control practitioner; I cared for patients with tuberculosis. Now I was infected.

I knew that studies showed that patients in isolation see hospital staff less frequently because staff members don't want to wear the protective gear necessary to enter the patients' rooms. Just at a time when I was hoping for a visit from family and friends. Afraid and alone, I thought of an old hymn.

Suddenly, I was back at my dear friend Anna's funeral, singing an old hymn that had been a healing balm for the both of us: "It Is Well with My Soul." I sang right out loud to the Only One Who could hear me.
—ROBERTA MESSNER

> *When peace like a river attendeth my way,*
> *When sorrows like sea billows roll;*
> *Whatever my lot, Thou hast taught me to say:*
> *It is well, it is well with my soul.*

When you're feeling all alone, sing a favorite old hymn, albeit off-key, at the top of your lungs. Your Savior will adore your heartfelt worship.

INADEQUATE NO MORE

Watch the road; strengthen your back, summon all your strength.
—NAHUM 2:1 (NAS)

MY HUSBAND AND I HAD DRIVEN EAST FOR A TEN-DAY VISIT WITH OUR children, and just about the time we planned to leave for home, Leo suddenly developed a serious foot infection. We knew from previous bouts that to treat it required daily intravenous antibiotics. Back home in Winnipeg, that just meant an easy five-minute drive to the nearest hospital; in Toronto, it meant a hasty visit to a local walk-in clinic, where a doctor prescribed pills to stave off the infection while we drove home.

The next morning as I got into the driver's seat, I was keenly aware and not a little anxious that ahead of me lay 1,200 miles of winding, hilly roads through northern Ontario's wilderness. We usually take turns driving, but this time most of the responsibility would fall on me.

Leaving behind the bustling traffic of Toronto and nosing the car northward, deeper and deeper into a beautiful landscape of trees and lakes and rocks and hills, I felt my anxiety slowly disappear. I was especially thankful for a special feature in the driver's seat that could be adjusted to alleviate my aching back.

We arrived home safely on the third day, and while Leo's infection was successfully treated, I, too, was healed—of those niggling fears of inadequacy with which I'd begun the journey. —ALMA BARKMAN

> *Thank You, Lord, that I can draw on my experience and*
> *Your strength to help me over the next hurdle.*

In the car or on the bus or train, before you start moving, whisper a self-affirmation.

GOD HAS ANSWERS OF HIS OWN

You are the God who performs miracles; you display your power among the peoples.
—PSALM 77:14 (NIV)

FOR TWO YEARS, MEDICATION HAD BEEN SUCCESSFUL IN HELPING OUR DAUGHTER Maria manage her Crohn's disease, minimizing the flare-ups of colon pain. Then, when she began eighth grade, the medication stopped working and she experienced intense pain that was debilitating and unpredictable. She missed a lot of school, and by Christmas break she was in the hospital.

I'd been praying for her all through her illness, but I decided I hadn't been bold enough. I would pray for a miracle. Her doctor was talking to us about a stronger medication, but we were scared of possible side effects. So every day I told God, "I'm praying for a miracle for Maria."

Maria left the hospital feeling better, but nothing prevented the continuing flare-ups. I kept praying. Then one day I spoke with the mother of a teenage girl who had been taking the stronger medication for several months. The family had determined that the risks of the disease outweighed the risks of the medication. It seemed to work. "It's been a miracle treatment for us," the mother said.

I've been praying for a miracle healing for Maria, I thought, *but can't God also heal through the gift of medicine? Maybe this is our miracle.*

It was. The new medication helped Maria regain control of her life. And I learned a valuable lesson: Faith isn't about God giving me answers I want; it's about believing in His answers. —GINA BRIDGEMAN

Forgive me, Lord, for being so slow to trust You.
Thank You for Your unending love.

Tonight, when you retire and turn out your bedside light, ask God for faith that helps you trust Him in the dark.

PERSISTENCE IN PRAYERS

Immediately Jesus, perceiving in Himself that the power proceeding from Him had gone forth, turned around in the crowd and said, "Who touched My garments?"
—MARK 5:30 (NAS)

WHEN JESUS ASKED WHO HAD TOUCHED HIM IN THE CROWDED STREET, a woman fell trembling at His feet and confessed. For twelve years she'd suffered a worsening health condition, going broke paying physicians. She had pretty much given up until she heard about Jesus. She thought if she could just touch the fringe of His cloak, she would be made well.

Her plan was to sneak up behind Jesus in the press of people, reach out with a quick, furtive touch, and then disappear in the crowd. It almost worked. Only Jesus felt power leave Him at the same instant the woman felt her body heal. Her reach and Jesus's response met in a miraculous healing.

The Bible doesn't give her name, but I call her the fringe lady—faith reaching in God expectation. Jesus's parting words, "Go in peace and be healed of your affliction" (Mark 5:34, NAS), must have been a soothing salve for all of her remaining years.

The fringe lady's faith was desperate, even frightened—the way my faith gets when my best efforts have failed and I think I'm out of options. Yet Jesus commended her, saying, "Daughter, your faith has made you well" (Mark 5:34, NAS).

Wherever I am—however alone or exhausted or distraught—when I sincerely reach for Jesus, I know that He will respond to the barest touch.
—CAROL KNAPP

> *Holy Spirit, when I'm out of answers, help me to summon*
> *the faith to reach out for Jesus.*

Meditate on Mark 5:30 for five minutes. Then ask God to help you have the faith to be a "fringe lady."

FOCUSED PRAYERS

A woman…touched the hem of His garment. For she said to herself, "If only I may touch His garment, I shall be made well." —MATTHEW 9:20–21 (NKJV)

AFTER MY FRIEND PATRICIA RECEIVED A DISTRESSING DIAGNOSIS OF METASTASIZED cancer, I cooked, cleaned, and chauffeured for her. I also prayed, for her as well as for myself, but in a vague way that didn't feel meaningful—until I stopped and took a nap.

After lunch one day, I ran out of steam. Anticipating the rejuvenating power of a catnap, I pushed away from my computer and kicked off my shoes. As I stretched out on my bed, some garbled revision of the Matthew 9 "if only" passage came to mind: *"If only I could touch the edge of…sleep."*

I quickly nodded off. I awoke fifteen minutes later, refreshed physically, if not spiritually. But even before I opened my eyes, I felt the warmth of my tabby, Kitty, herself napping on the quilt. She'd rested her cheek on the back of my hand and extended her front paw across my shirt-cuffed wrist. Before I disturbed her pose or resumed my routine, I lingered a moment. Her quiet touch settled my spirit and coaxed the biblical "if only" from my memory: *"If only I may touch Jesus's garment."* It's a woman's faith-full prayer for health.

My prayers for Patricia—and myself—are more focused now. —EVELYN BENCE

Dear Jesus, be at our side to heal and guide.

Do you have a special need that is wearing you down today? During your prayer time, focus on the specifics of it and believe.

Father, I praise Your Holy Name
for answered prayer and for prayer
warriors. At some of the lowest points
of my life, I cried out to You for health,
healing, and deliverance. Thank You
that during my times of need,
I was covered with a blanket of prayer
from Your saints.

DOROTHY BANKSTON ADAMS

Chapter 2

WHEN YOU FACE TRIALS

....

Faith, I've concluded,
means believing in advance
what will only make sense in reverse.

FROM *THE QUESTION THAT NEVER GOES AWAY*
BY PHILIP YANCEY

ROCK-SOLID ADVICE

Praise be to the God and Father of our Lord Jesus Christ, who has blessed us in the heavenly realms with every spiritual blessing in Christ. —EPHESIANS 1:3 (NIV)

THIS SUMMER HAS BEEN EVENTFUL FOR MY FAMILY. WE'VE WELCOMED NEW babies. We've had cookouts and blown a million bubbles (mostly at two-year-old Isabelle Grace's request). We've watched grandson Mace blow out one candle on his birthday cake and eat (way too many) ice cream cones. Good times.

But some of the events haven't been joyful or welcome. My mother-in-law, Opal, was diagnosed with cancer. She spent the summer undergoing chemo at Vanderbilt Hospital in Nashville, Tennessee. They hoped the treatments would shrink the tumor, but the cancer continues to grow.

There have been other family problems too—some physical, some financial, others emotional. I wake each morning and pray for the overwhelming needs of those I love. I've even begun to wonder what new calamity might unfold. Which is why the sunflowers were a welcome surprise.

Twin stalks rise out of the flower bed near my sunroom. By the time I noticed them, they were knee-high and looked enough unlike a weed not to be pulled. They grew taller and soon I knew: I was going to have sunflowers!

As I admired these beauties this morning, I noticed a clump of red geraniums that surrounded a small gray rock, which simply read *Rejoice*.

Rock-solid advice. Because in the midst of a trial, there is always God's eternal love—and some unexpected blessings. —MARY LOU CARNEY

Keep me from being so downcast, Lord, that I forget
to look for the flowers lining my pathway.

 Spend time in a garden today and let your mind concentrate on God's beautiful work.

THE ONE TRUE THING

Jesus answered, "I am the way and the truth and the life…."
—JOHN 14:6 (NIV)

MY GRANDSON DRAKE AND I WERE STANDING OUTSIDE CHURCH ONE SUNDAY morning, waiting for the rest of the family to join us. I was, as is my custom, dressed up—a lacy top, a gauze broomstick skirt, and a great straw hat with a band of tulle and a cluster of silk hydrangeas. Suddenly, it started to sprinkle. "Oh no," I wailed. "My beautiful hat will get wet!"

Drake looked at me, considering this for a moment. Then, with perfect three-year-old logic, he said, "Nana, your flowers will like it. They need rain!"

I laughed, even as the drops became thicker. All Drake knew about flowers was that they needed water. He wasn't aware that silk blossoms this perpetually full could be had for $3.99 at craft stores.

Knowing what's real and what's not is pretty much a lifelong quest, whether you're seeking true love, testing the waters of a new friendship, or choosing which tub of butter-like substance to buy. I'd like to say that age has made me an expert at sniffing out the fakes in life—the friend who will desert you just after you tell her your dearest secret or the designer blouse that frays the third time you wear it—but I still make mistakes in judgment.

I have learned to cling tightly to those things that have proven themselves good and true: my husband, Gary; my family; my closest friends; and, most of all, my faith. There's nothing fake or fleeting about the way God has seen me through the traumas and temptations of my life. —MARY LOU CARNEY

In this world of confusing decisions and clamoring options,
You, Lord, are the one true thing.

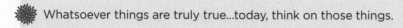 Whatsoever things are truly true…today, think on those things.

WAITING HOPEFULLY

What is your life? You are a mist that appears for a little while and then vanishes.
—James 4:14 (NIV)

MOST OF MY LIFE HAS BEEN SPENT WAITING. WHETHER I'M ON THE PHONE with the phone company (oh, the irony!), pondering whether my boyfriend would ever propose (he did and we married in 2009!), or just sitting at a red light, wait I must.

This year has been a trial in waiting. I waited to learn if my job would evaporate. I waited to hear from God if now was the time to expand our family. I waited three weeks for a piece of mail that finally arrived with no apparent reason for its delay.

Each time I'm forced to wait, I remind myself of a quote that I read online: "In Spanish, the verbs 'to wait' and 'to hope' are the same: *esperar.* Waiting is negative; hoping is positive. So try to wait with hope. This will help you remember that you're on your way to something worth waiting for."

How often do I wait with my arms crossed, foot tapping, an eye roll cued up and ready to go? How many hours have I wasted with my eyes narrowed on the clock? A life of frustration is not what God wants for me. God calls me to share love, to seek others, and to rejoice in creation.

Our moments here are not promised, but they are precious—and I plan to embrace each one. —ASHLEY KAPPEL

Lord, I praise You in Your great wisdom. Even across languages,
Your Word speaks volumes and brings light unto my path,
teaching me to wait hopefully.

Are you forced to wait in a matter? Find something to hope for in the situation.

GOD'S IMPROVISATION

Never be lacking in zeal, but keep your spiritual fervor, serving the Lord.
—ROMANS 12:11 (NIV)

A FRIEND OF MINE TOLD ME ABOUT AN EXERCISE SHE LEARNED IN AN improvisation class. It's called "Yes…and," and it works something like this: A student calls out an idea for an improv, such as "We're kittens." Instead of dismissing the idea as dumb, another student must respond with an additional idea, saying, "Yes…and we're prehistoric!" Each student adds an idea to expand the skit and nobody knows where the whole thing is going.

I wondered if the same idea might work for me when facing God's challenges, especially the ones that I might be more inclined to avoid than enthusiastically embrace. So when our pastor announced that our church was planning a health fair for a low-income, inner-city neighborhood, my immediate reaction was *I'm not a doctor or nurse. What can I do?* But instead I said, "Yes…and I'll work wherever you need help." I was assigned to the registration table, and not only did I put my organizational skills to good use, I even used a little of my high school Spanish. I also had fun and finished the day knowing that I'd helped people get information and services that they really needed.

Now when God sends a challenge my way, I fight the urge to say "No" and instead say "Yes…and." I think of it as God's improvisation. His ideas may surprise me, but I can relax and follow His lead because He always knows where things are going. —GINA BRIDGEMAN

Lord, open my mind to the many ways that
You think I can serve You.

 Make sure your yeses are God's yeses today.

BEING REFINED

"I have refined you, though not as silver; I have tested you in the furnace of affliction." —ISAIAH 48:10 (NIV)

MY CAT HAD A HACKING COUGH; I THOUGHT IT WAS A HAIRBALL. TWO HUNDRED and thirty-eight dollars later, I learned it was a respiratory infection. "You'll want liquid antibiotics, right?" my veterinarian asked. "Even though they cost more."

My empty checking account leered at me. "No, I'll give Prince a pill."

He lifted one eyebrow. "Twice a day for two weeks? You can't miss a day."

"I can do it," I said.

I switched from praying nightly for my cat to recover to praying that I would live through this. I put a tablet in with his food; he ate around it. I mixed it with liver (his favorite); he left it so long, it developed a crust.

When I finally got the medicine down his throat, I cried, "Yes!" and let him go—only to find the tiny white pill in the corner of the room. He knocked over the TV table, he pulled down a curtain; now I was late for work again.

"You're part of a team," my manager scolded as she wrote me up—again. "I know that you're a good employee, so getting a reprimand must be a hard pill to swallow."

"What did you just say?" I asked. It clicked! I'd just received something that would make me better.

"I'll be on time from now on," I promised. And I was. —LINDA NEUKRUG

God, is there a change I need to make that's a "hard pill to swallow"? Let me see it as an opportunity to make myself what You think I can be.

Think back to a time when God helped you tackle a difficult change. Have joy in remembering.

A SWEET GIFT

Now some of the scribes were sitting there, questioning in their hearts, "Why does this man speak thus? It is blasphemy! Who can forgive sins but God alone?"
—MARK 2:6–7 (RSV)

WHEN I WAS DIVORCED SOME YEARS AGO, I NEEDED THE LOVE AND SUPPORT of my old high school youth-group leaders. I hadn't seen them in years and was living in another state, but when I contacted them I was in for a rude awakening. Their harsh condemnation was crushing, and ever after I carried a deep sense of grief and loss.

Last year I returned to Arizona, where I went to high school, for the first time in thirty-eight years. When Gwen, one of the youth-group leaders, heard I was coming, she asked to see me. I wasn't sure I wanted to see her.

Waiting for her at my friend Carol's house, I paced the floor. I was determined to tell her about my feelings, but I wasn't sure how to handle it. I'd never stopped loving Gwen, and her condemnation was a badly healed scar.

To my surprise, when Gwen came up the walk, I saw her beautiful smile, a smile I've never forgotten. She gave me a well-remembered hug, and before I could catch my breath, she gave me a warm and weepy apology. Her words to me had been bothering her for years, she said, and she was so grateful to God for giving her the opportunity to tell me how sorry she was. "I was young, I was brainless, I followed the script. Will you forgive me?" she asked.

Forgive Gwen? Sometimes forgiveness is so easy. —BRENDA WILBEE

Thank You, God, for never forgetting our grief and loss,
and for the healing power of forgiveness born of You.

Has someone in your past hurt you with a pain that lingers to this day? Do something unexpected and kind on their behalf.

COMPASSIONATE JESUS

But even so, you have done right in helping me in my present difficulty.
—PHILIPPIANS 4:14 (TLB)

A SAVAGE TORNADO HIT GREENSBURG, KANSAS, A COUPLE OF YEARS AGO. Almost every house and business was destroyed, power and water supplies were cut, and most of the 1,500 residents were left homeless.

People and churches from all over the country responded quickly and with overwhelming generosity. Teams of workers, supplies, and cleanup equipment poured into the area. Living in Kansas, my husband, Don, and I weren't directly impacted, but we wanted to help. We prayed, of course, and donated to the disaster fund. But I wanted to do more.

My uncertainty lasted until I heard the Greensburg disaster report at a church conference. The bishop asked us to take home three images:

1. Scripture, because God's Word shapes our lives and leads our hearts.
2. Church connection, because in three short weeks money for rebuilding had poured in from all over the world.
3. A toothbrush, to remind us to give with our heads as well as our hearts.

On-site responders who can offer real assistance and comfort are essential in helping people recover from any disaster. But money and prayers for those who have experienced loss and those who aid rebuilding are valuable gifts too.
—PENNEY SCHWAB

Compassionate Jesus, teach me to give generously,
thoughtfully, and with compassion.

Read the front page of your newspaper. Find a family who has gone through a loss (a fire or a flood, maybe). Take them a bag of groceries or a couple of boxes of disposable diapers if there are babies involved. (If money is short, get creative with coupons.)

LET THE SYMBOL GO

*A time to get, and a time to lose... —*ECCLESIASTES 3:6 (KJV)

WHEN MY HUSBAND, ROBERT, PROPOSED TO ME, HE GAVE ME A NECKLACE WITH two pearls, each one set on a gold strand. The two strands intertwined as a symbol of our lasting love. It became my most precious possession.

Six years later, I fell from a porch, badly twisting my back. At the hospital I was asked to remove my necklace for X-rays. I handed it to Robert.

We returned home and realized my necklace was gone. Robert looked everywhere without finding it. I cried myself to sleep but awoke with these words: *God has given you true love. You have the real thing! Let the symbol go!*

Is this what Solomon meant when he wrote "a time to get and a time to lose"? As I wait in prayer, this answer comes:

In the far vaster order beyond time,
nothing is ever truly lost.
It's safe to let go
with tranquility and trust,
for your truest treasures
are forever preserved for you
in eternity.

I wouldn't be honest if I said I no longer have moments of sadness about the loss of my necklace and the many other worldly things we lost. But whenever I have a loss, I sit in prayer and say, "With God's help, I can let go." And I find that most of the time I can. —MARILYN MORGAN KING

> *Bountiful Creator, help me to see my losses as temporal and*
> *my treasures as eternal.*

 Give something gifted to you to a member of the next generation.

FACING DREADED TASKS

For the Lord will be at your side and will keep your foot from being snared.
—PROVERBS 3:26 (NIV)

THE PLACE I FIND IT HARDEST TO ACT LIKE A GOOD PERSON OF FAITH IS AT the Laundromat. I visit once a year during spring cleaning at our beach rental house. I come in staggering under enough bedspreads, mattress covers, and blankets to do eleven loads in the biggest super-duper washers they have.

I realized I had a serious problem the year I pushed my cart over to the dryer and came back and found a retired couple using my yellow bottle of detergent that I'd left on top of the washer. Of course I said something to them, and they had the audacity to act like it was theirs! Five minutes later, I discovered *my* bottle of detergent hidden under dirty blankets in my cart. I apologized but felt like dirty clothes inside.

After that, I started praying before my Laundromat trips. And I'm always glad because my character is usually tested in some new way. One year a stranger told me she wanted to get out of an abusive relationship when the man she was arguing with left to get change. I wasn't sure if she was sincere or not, but I prayed with her and slipped her the number of a local abuse hotline

This year I was sorely tested by a woman who let her two girls chase each other around the table where I was trying to fold queen-size bedspreads. I learned to remember my past mistakes when I'm in a place where my worst side usually comes out. —KAREN BARBER

Dear Father, here's the place and situation that brings out the worst in me.
I need Your help, so I can be a good person when I'm there. Amen.

If there's a place that brings out the worst in you, "pray up" before you go there. Expectantly await God's intervention.

YOU ARE PRECIOUS TO GOD

The Spirit of the Lord God is upon me.... He hath sent me to bind up the brokenhearted.... —ISAIAH 61:1 (KJV)

"HOW'S JOHN DOING?" A WOMAN FROM MY PRAYER GROUP ASKED. I HADN'T talked to her in a while. We had changed my son's anxiety medication, and instead of improving, my twelve-year-old spent two weeks in the hospital.

"He's up and down. Some days he is fine. Other days he seems fine, and a minute later we're wondering if we should call nine-one-one."

She paused, then gently said, "The unpredictability must be hard."

It was my turn to pause. "Yes," I said, "but I don't focus as much on that now. What I'm finally beginning to grasp is learning to say *thank You* each day my son is alive." Another pause. "It took me a long time to get there," I added.

"How do your other kids handle it?" my friend asked.

"They pretty much know to go to another room and entertain themselves when John starts to blow. They enjoy him when he's able to be fun and keep themselves safe when he's not."

"I'll keep praying for you."

"Thanks. It's hard, but it's harder to be John. He's a great kid with really difficult problems. I wish he could know just how precious he is to God."

My friend nodded. There wasn't much else to say, but a lot to pray for.
—JULIA ATTAWAY

Lord, people suffer. Let me hold them up to You before I cry out for myself.

Think of those in your life with problems. Write their names on a sticky note as a reminder to pray for them this week.

FINDING FORGIVENESS

Father, forgive them; for they know not what they do.... —LUKE 23:34 (KJV)

I FLEW TO JAPAN IN 1974 TO MEET A MAN I'D HATED FOR THIRTY YEARS—the commander who led the infamous attack on Pearl Harbor.

Mitsuo Fuchida, a small man of seventy-two, met me at my hotel in Kyoto. As a translator repeated his words, I saw a boy dreaming of serving his emperor by driving Western colonial powers out of Asia. "When we lost the war, most of my officers committed suicide. But I had a wife and children." He moved them to a farm. As he worked the fields, news of the war crimes trials in Tokyo came over the radio. "It was then I learned about atrocities in our prisoner-of-war camps." I sensed the horror and disillusionment of this man.

In a train station, someone handed him a leaflet written by an American ex-prisoner of war. "But...the American wrote that he loved us! The Japanese who'd tortured him!" This was because, the leaflet said, Jesus did.

Fuchida recognized that name: Jesus was one of the gods of the enemy. Fuchida bought a Bible and, discovered there were not many gods but One, Who loved all people; Who came to earth as a common man; Who said as He was crucified, "Father, forgive them, for they know not what they do."

"Why then...this Jesus had prayed for me too!" Tears trembled in his eyes. By now I was fighting tears too.

Conversion made him a traitor; he and his wife still received death threats. "We do not care. It is better to die and be with Jesus." —ELIZABETH SHERRILL

Father, forgive my unforgivingness.

Tell yourself you forgive a person who has upset you. Repeat it out loud until the message is received in your heart.

TRUST UNSHAKABLE

"Here on earth you will have many trials and sorrows. But take heart, because I have overcome the world." —JOHN 16:33 (NLT)

ROSE KENNEDY HAS GIVEN US A LEGACY OF FAITH AND COURAGE, AND I frequently find myself inspired by the strength she showed throughout her life.

I was desperately trying to hold together the raw and ragged edges of a hurt that wouldn't knit itself together and heal. My thoughts were jumbled by grief and tears. Then came a lifeline from Mrs. Kennedy, who said, "It's not the tears that make the pain more bearable; it's determination!" *Determination.* That one word gave me stamina, resolve, and resilience.

As a young girl, during the contemplative moments of a Lenten retreat, Mrs. Kennedy thought of the joys and sorrows, difficulties and griefs that inevitably come into all our lives. Whatever happened, she determined, "I will hold my soul forever free!" She refused to let her faith be bound by circumstance; instead, she placed unshakable trust in the goodness of God.

Keeping in motion gave her emotional ventilation. Daily she plunged into the waters of Cape Cod for a swim and then walked and prayed. She made up her mind to not be defeated by the tragedy of losing three sons. Senator Edward Kennedy said of her, "Mother believes that if there are rays of sunshine in a stormy sky, focus on the light, not the darkness."

On Rose Kennedy's birthday, I give thanks for her example of strength.
—FAY ANGUS

When I'm twisted up with worry, set my soul free, Steady my faith, strengthen my heart, and wrap me in Your gift of peace.

Is there someone who has inspired you? Find out their birth date and pray for them (or their loved ones) all day long.

PATIENT ANSWERS FOR
PERSISTENT PLEAS

Don't you realize how kind, tolerant, and patient God is with you?
—ROMANS 2:4 (NLT)

TODAY I WAS WITH MY TWENTY-TWO-MONTH-OLD GRANDSON, BROCK, feeding him his lunch. Between bites, he asked me the same questions over and over. Bite of cheese. "Nana, where Mama?" Bite of turkey. "Nana, where Papa?" Bite of bread and butter. "Elmo? Elmo?"

The first two I could answer: "At work." The Elmo one I winged: "Yes, Elmo."

Brock took a drink of milk and then began again. "Nana, where Mama?" "Nana, where Papa?" "Elmo? Elmo?"

I gave the same answers. Our conversation took on a predictable rhythm.

I thought about Brock's incessant questions as I drove home and was reminded of someone else who asks the same questions over and over—me. And the recipient of this repetitive babble? God.

Year after year I ask, "Why don't You answer my prayers?" "Where are You when I hurt?" "Why must my family face this trial?"

The same answers come: *I hear you. Trust Me. I love you just as you are.*

If God tires of my endlessly repeated questions, He never shows it. I guess patience is something God—and nanas—have in common.

—MARY LOU CARNEY

Open my ears and my heart, Lord, that I might hear and believe
Your patient answers to my persistent pleas.

Climb up into God's big lap and ask Him a question you've asked Him many times before. He won't mind. In fact, He'll revel in your presence.

ENJOY THE JOURNEY

And they began to speak against God and Moses. "Why have you brought us out of Egypt to die here in the wilderness?" they complained. "There is nothing to eat here and nothing to drink. And we hate this horrible manna!" —NUMBERS 21:5 (NLT)

THE DIGITAL MAP TOLD ME OUR DRIVE TO DISNEYLAND WOULD LAST EIGHT hours. With two kids in the backseat and my wife by my side, we left early.

The map didn't tell me was how tedious the drive would be: flat countryside with few good stops. Around hour three, "Are we there yet?" began.

"Yes," I said, "get out now." The kids laughed.

Two hours later, I could not find the humor. Every whiny syllable spiked my blood pressure. My normally delightful children were gnawing on my last nerve. I thought of Moses in the wilderness. Two million followers delivering forty years of grousing. His frustration level had to have been high.

As the "Happiest Place on Earth" drew closer, I was about to lay in to the urchins, when the Holy Spirit asked, *Bill, what if you sound like that to God?*

I thought of my boatload of unanswered prayers. The trials I thought I didn't deserve. *Lord, have You brought me here just to torment me?* Had my prayers devolved into a sanctimonious equivalent of "Are we there yet?"

I whispered my apology to God.

"Are we there yet?" the kids asked again.

I swallowed my planned rebuke. "Two more hours," I said. "But who wants ice cream?" —BILL GIOVANNETTI

Lord, teach me to enjoy the journey and trust Your map,
no matter how long, painful, twisty, or boring the road may be.

 Take a ride in the country today with no destination in mind, only joy.

WALKING UPHILL JOYFULLY

The hills are clothed with gladness. —PSALM 65:12 (NIV)

AT APPROXIMATELY 7:35 EVERY WEEKDAY MORNING, MAGGIE, MARY, STEPHEN, and I begin to descend the 129 steps of 187th Street that bring us down to Broadway. Then we walk up to the girls' school at the top of the opposite hill.

At the bottom of the first hill, we meet crowds of Orthodox Jewish children on their way to *yeshiva*. Then up the second hill into a swirl of Hispanic parents and kids, some heading in our direction, others bound for the school on the corner. Snatches of conversation come our way as Maggie runs to catch up with a friend: a child argues that he doesn't need a scarf, another cries over forgotten homework, a grandmother gives a last-minute lecture.

At the school door Stephen and I say good-bye to the girls, and then it's down the hill and up the hill to go home. Six and a half hours later, we set out again, to pick up our pupils. School has been good for our leg muscles.

At the end of the day, Maggie tells me what she couldn't eat from her lunch box, whether or not she got a sticker, and who in her first-grade class is behaving better. Mary reports on what happened at recess, how annoying her classmate Anthony was, and which test she has the next day.

Stephen races ahead. We cross Broadway and decide whether to walk up the hill or detour a few blocks south and take the subway elevator up.

At home the girls change out of their uniforms and sit down to do their homework. The hills wait patiently for another day. —JULIA ATTAWAY

Lord, let me walk every hill—whether to school or to Calvary—
with my eyes open to see the world as You do.

Make every day Easter in your heart as you thank Jesus for His example of facing trials with faith.

SIMPLE GRATITUDE

"Do not be anxious about tomorrow...."—MATTHEW 6:34 (RSV)

MY DERMATOLOGIST REMOVED A SKIN LESION FROM MY ARM AND SENT IT to a lab to be tested. He was worried about its appearance, and the fact that he was worried scared me.

Through the fog of deep sleep, I heard my phone ring this morning. Grabbing it, I saw that the call was from my doctor. My heart lurched and my blood pressure soared. I croaked a weak hello. "Scott, I've got good news. Lab report says it's a pre-skin cancer. Nothing to worry about. Glad we got right on it and things look good."

Now, several hours later, I am taking it all in, profoundly grateful for life. But I am sixty-two years old and no one lives forever. I will face a day when the news is not good, when my fears are real, when health breaks down, when mortality grasps my hand and will not let go. So I ask, "What has this new lease on life taught me?"

Above all, I affirm that each day I live will be acknowledged as a pure gift, a moment of time that is unique, unrepeatable, and must be savored. Second, I resolve to live each day with one primary purpose: to show love to at least one other child of God, animals included! And, finally, the greatest gift I can offer to God is my heartfelt thanksgiving. For it is simple gratitude that is the most healing medicine known to humankind, and it is thanksgiving that transcends all time and death. —SCOTT WALKER

Father, fill this day with love and gratitude. Amen.

Gratitude is the heart's memory. Make a wooden plate for the bottom of your front door in which you list twenty things your family is grateful for. (Use a paint pen.)

BUILDING A CHILD'S FAITH

For as the heavens are higher than the earth, so are my ways higher than your ways and my thoughts than your thoughts. —ISAIAH 55:9 (RSV)

SOLOMON, MY FIVE-YEAR-OLD, GETS UPSET BY THINGS THAT DON'T FOLLOW the rules of cause-and-effect. So when Faith, a classmate of his, was diagnosed with leukemia, Solomon tried to make sense of it all. "Why did this happen?" "Why is Faith too tired to play?" "Why did she lose her curls?" "Will she die?"

At that moment I longed for the innocent "What's that?" of Solomon's toddler years. How could I explain that sometimes bad things happen for unknown reasons that I found myself hugging Solomon, thankful that he was healthy.

"I don't know why Faith got leukemia. I don't think anyone knows," I said.

Solomon's face perked up. "Mommy, I know who knows."

"Who?" I asked.

"God. God knows everything. He's got a plan."

"You're right," I said.

"But, Mommy, how can we figure it out? How can we know the plan?"

"I don't think we can. But we can pray for Faith and her family."

"Oh, okay," he said. "I have another question."

"Okay."

"How come the teacher never picks me to be line leader?"

I'm happy to say that Faith's leukemia is in remission. Aptly named, Faith has filled us all with hope and gratitude. —SABRA CIANCANELLI

Dear Lord, when there are no answers,
let me always trust Your plan.

 Acknowledge the fact that God's ways are not our ways by surrendering something to Him that you've been holding on to too long.

GOD SEES YOU THROUGH

"To give light to those who sit in darkness and in the shadow of death, to guide our feet into the way of peace." —LUKE 1:79 (RSV)

"THAT'S GOOD NEWS," SAID MY COLLEAGUE. "SO YOU'RE GOING BACK TO WORK!"

"I hate to ask you this," I replied, "but what floor is our office on?"

"No worries," she said calmly. "It's on the fourth floor."

Forgetting the location of your office is a chilling experience. And that was just the beginning of the legacy of electroconvulsive therapy. It vanquishes depression, but as depression exits, often memory follows right behind. I could look at the future without flinching, but pieces of my life were gone—forever.

"I'm so sorry I missed it," I said to my husband when he mentioned a memorial service for a friend.

"You were there with me," he replied, looking startled.

The blessing—and there is one—is that some of the memory of how depression had driven me into a dark corner was gone, along with the memory of hospital visits and how to start the car. I pieced some of it together from my notebook and relearned the details of a job I had done for years.

Never have the words *guiding light* meant so much. God tests no limits. He asks for no records and needs no introduction. I couldn't pray my way out of depression, however hard I tried. But the prayers of others kept me safe and the unconditional love of God brought me through. —BRIGITTE WEEKS

*Dear Lord, give me the patience to learn my life anew and
the spirit to rejoice in Your light.*

Personalize Psalm 118:24: "This is the day *my* Lord hath made. *I* will rejoice and be glad in it."

TRUST LIKE A CHILD

"In quietness and trust is your strength...." —ISAIAH 30:15 (NIV)

MY DAUGHTER KENDALL AND HER HUSBAND, DAVID, HAD THEIR FIRST BABY recently and spent several weeks both elated and exhausted by the new reality.

"Why don't you let me be your night nanny tonight?" I offered one afternoon. They readily agreed.

So that night I jokingly donned the hospital scrubs I'd worn during Kendall's C-section delivery and kissed my husband good-bye. As I drove to their house, I felt a bit smug about the great gift I was about to give them.

When Kendall and David saw me dressed for my shift, they rolled their bleary eyes and took an obligatory picture. Soon they settled me into the guest room with my precious eight-pound charge. "Don't worry about a thing," I said.

I got ready for bed, checked my supplies and the sleeping baby beside me, and then turned off the light. In the darkness my own worries started filling my mind—worries that always seemed to grow bigger at night. Then a new one struck me: I couldn't hear the baby breathing. I snapped on the light, saw his tiny chest peacefully moving up and down, and turned the light back off.

That's how the night went. Twice, I jumped up at his first stirrings to meet his needs—feeding, burping, changing—and rocked him back to sleep.

As sunlight peeked through the curtains, I found myself watching him sleeping. I'd come here to give my daughter a gift of sleep, but I received the greater gift: a reminder of the trust I should have for all my needs. —CAROL KUYKENDALL

Lord, a sleeping baby is a gift that reminds me of You.

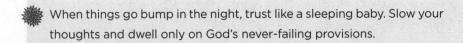

When things go bump in the night, trust like a sleeping baby. Slow your thoughts and dwell only on God's never-failing provisions.

I've made mistakes. My hair is turning gray. My youth is gone, and my beauty has disappeared. The kids are grown, and there's no looking back. I was foolish in my younger days. That's not the way I wanted to do it. But You were working in my life, molding and shaping. You have brought me through, and taught me much. I'm thankful for the gift of wisdom that comes with time.

PATRICIA L. SMITH

Chapter 3

WHEN YOU FEEL AFRAID

·····················

*Courage is born at the point
where God's grace and human
effort intersect.*

FROM *THE DISCERNMENT OF SPIRITS*
BY FATHER TIMOTHY M. GALLAGHER

GROWING IN FAITH

"The one who had received the one talent went off and dug a hole in the ground and hid his master's money." —MATTHEW 25:18 (NRSV)

MY HUSBAND, KRIS, AND I ARE OF DIFFERENT BENTS REGARDING PLANNING. He loves considering best-case, worst-case, and likeliest-case scenarios.

I despise planning. Planning evokes all the terrors fermenting below the surface of my faith. I don't like thinking about retirement or the loan needed to pay for the girls' schooling, much less talking about it. My go-to response is fear! In my view, the guy in Jesus's parable who buries his master's money is not lazy but terrified. If it were up to me, we'd never discuss the future.

Not that I'm more trusting than Kris. When problems arise—as they do, despite our plans—Kris's mustard seed is definitely bigger than mine. "God will take care of us," he says. Planning is part of letting God do just that.

Kris likes a joke in which a drowning man turns down help from a rowboat, then a speedboat, then a helicopter, saying, "God will rescue me." Later, in heaven, he asks God why He didn't answer that prayer.

God responds, "I sent you a rowboat, then a speedboat, then a helicopter..."

Planning, Kris argues, is good stewardship of the opportunities God sends. I fear I'll never learn this, but I keep trying. —PATTY KIRK

Father, help me remember not only Your provision but
Your expectations of us as its stewards. Replace my fears with
good judgment and ever-growing trust.

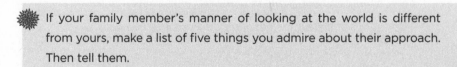

If your family member's manner of looking at the world is different from yours, make a list of five things you admire about their approach. Then tell them.

GOD'S UNSEEN PROTECTION

"It laughs at fear, afraid of nothing; it does not shy away from the sword."
—JOB 39:22 (NIV)

COLBY, MY GOLDEN RETRIEVER, POUNDED THROUGH THE WOODS, ENJOYING his first visit to Blue Ridge, Georgia. We turned down a gravel lane that looped by several houses perched high above the water when, suddenly, Colby froze.

The high-pitched whine emanating from the back of his throat was his only giveaway. My eyes followed to where his gaze locked: our neighbor's life-sized, two-dimensional metal cutout of a bear.

From where we stood, the bear looked to be crossing a stream a few yards away from us. Had Colby noticed the bear a few feet earlier or later, he would've seen what I knew to be true: This harmless, flat, rusted bear was only a lawn ornament. Instead, Colby cowered and whimpered until I carried him far enough along the path so that he could recognize the bear was only metal.

I often wonder how many times God has had to pull me past certain trials that I don't notice until I'm knee-deep in them and cowering. If I'd seen them coming or had the patience to wait until the fear subsided, I might've been better prepared to call out to God in prayer. Instead, I collapsed in a pile of woe and wailing, panicked at the situation I faced.

When I comfort Colby when he encounters something scary, I remember that God comforts me. I may not be able to see the leash, but if I pay attention, I can feel the tug on my heart. —ASHLEY KAPPEL

Lord, remind me that giving in to my fear only allows it to bloom.
Remind me to follow You out of the darkness and into the light.

Set your alarm clock to wake you up before dawn. Remember, the darkest hour means dawn is just in sight.

HE WILL NEVER LEAVE YOU

"I will not leave you desolate; I will come to you." —John 14:18 (RSV)

I opened my eyes to total blackness. I had to go to the bathroom, now! My feet slammed onto the floor. *Why is the bed so low? Oh yeah, we're in Fairhope, Alabama, in a bed-and-breakfast.*

Feeling my way, I remembered a recent doctor's visit. "You've lost a third of your sight in six weeks," he'd said. Or had he said hearing?

I felt a wave of terror. If I lost both my hearing and my sight, I'd be alone.

A familiar Voice whispered, *Keith, can you hear Me?*

"Yes, Sir," I said, very relieved. "I'm glad You're still with me."

I'll always be with you. But what will you do if you can't see or hear?

"Maybe You could help me tell my family I'm all right. Maybe I could figure out how to help people like me surrender to You."

How did you think of that in the midst of your own fear?

"Well, Sir, remember in 1956, after my mother's graveside service when I realized that I was alone? You asked me, *What are you going to do?* I said, 'Maybe You can show me how to introduce other lonely people to You.'"

So that's what your work has really been about.

"Yes, Sir, I guess so."

Then I heard my wife, Andrea. "Keith, are you all right?"

"Yeah, I'm okay."

"Can't you find the light switch?"

I smiled in the darkness. "Yeah, honey. I just did." —Keith Miller

Lord, thank You for sending the Light to guide us.

 Stop talking to God about how big your fears are. Rather, begin talking to your fears about how big your God is.

STRENGTHENING YOUR FAITH

I prayed to the Lord my God and made confession.... —Daniel 9:4 (NRSV)

"Bless me, Father, for I have sinned."

I make a practice of going to confession every year. I was raised a Catholic and maintain this discipline because I think it's important to humble myself before another person and to publicly acknowledge my sins and ask God's forgiveness.

"I feel that my faith is not strong enough," I said haltingly, "because sometimes I let fear overwhelm it."

"And you think that's a sin?" the priest asked.

"I do."

"You know," he said, "faith and fear are not opposites."

I looked surprised.

"Think about it," he said. "Fear is natural to us, part of our survival instinct. Fear is often a physical sensation: the hair rises on our arms, our pulse races, we get a metallic taste in our mouth. Faith is not physical. By being afraid, you don't displace faith. Fear can drive you toward your faith, for comfort and understanding. Not only can they coexist, fear can strengthen faith."

I didn't say a word, but the priest watched my expression closely. He smiled. "I can tell you're going to work on this, but no hurry. It can take a lifetime." —Marci Alborghetti

Merciful God, help me to remember that the only thing I have to fear is not fear itself but the loss of my perspective in You.

 Designate a special place in your home where you can focus on God every day. (Hint: It doesn't have to be a prayer closet.)

GOD IS EVER-PRESENT

"My God, my rock, in whom I take refuge...." —2 SAMUEL 22:3 (RSV)

OUR CAT CHI WAS BARELY SIX WEEKS OLD WHEN WE BROUGHT HER INTO OUR home in Los Angeles. No sooner had we done so than we started getting the house ready for an eventual sale. For the first two years of Chi's life, we packed several boxes of "clutter" a week and moved them out to the garage. Books and bookcases vanished. Furniture changed locations. Chi would hesitate in the doorway of a room as if she thought the floor might have changed too. We hoped she would realize we were the constant presence, even as the background shifted, but she was very nervous.

When we began showing the house, Chi would have to be crated until they left. Repeated confinement was not to her liking. After a week the house sold and she had uninterrupted freedom again, but the packing accelerated. The moving van showed up, and the house was suddenly empty. Chi was completely flummoxed.

On the two nights we spent in motels on our drive north, she wouldn't come out of her crate. And when we reached our new home, the entire upstairs was being remodeled, so we had to move into the basement for three months. She was just getting used to that when the upstairs was done, and we moved up there. Three years after that final move, Chi finally relaxed.

I, too, am hesitant when the landscape of my life changes. And just as I hoped Chi would understand that we were still there, I tell myself that there's a constant for me: God's presence. —RHODA BLECKER

> *Help me not to forget that You're there,*
> *Lord, no matter what else isn't.*

 Read 2 Samuel 22:3. Focus on the sweetly comforting word *refuge*.

BE A FRIEND TO LIGHT THE WAY

"I will rescue my flock...." —EZEKIEL 34:10 (NIV)

I MET PASTOR JOHN IN 1994. WE HAD BOTH JOINED ANIMAS FIRE DEPARTMENT, so I knew him as a friend before I began attending his church. One of our first calls was a mobile home on fire. When we arrived at the scene, there was some residual smoke but no flames. The fire started near a gas hot-water heater and melted a copper fitting on one of the water pipes. The resulting leak put out the fire.

Several veteran firefighters clapped me on the back and said, "Don't worry, Tim. You can put out the next one." It felt good to belong, to be with my new friends. We rolled up the hose lines and put away our air packs.

Most men, full of unspent adrenaline and gathered around a fire truck, do not readily take notice of other people. But John is not like most men. He had taken off his helmet and was talking to a young child. Reading fear in his eyes, John asked the little boy, "Were you scared?" The child didn't say anything, but he buried his head in John's gear and cried.

I never forgot that lesson. A church is not that different from a fire department. It's easy to fall into conversation with friends and ignore those people who aren't familiar, but now I do my best to seek out and comfort those who might be lonely or hurting or scared. —TIM WILLIAMS

Thank You, God, for giving me a pastor and
a friend to light my way.

 At your church service, search out someone who may be hurting. Invite them to join you for a cup of coffee or tea.

NATURE'S LESSON IN FAITH

Now faith is the substance of things hoped for, the evidence of things not seen.
—HEBREWS 11:1 (KJV)

THANK YOU, LORD, FOR PURPLE MARTINS! IT'S A PRAYER THAT ESCAPES MY LIPS over and over as I watch blue-black North American swallows catch wind currents and glide effortlessly through the sky. I hear their song and rush out to find them flying around the birdhouse at the edge of my pond.

"My birds are back!" I shout with joy to any neighbor within earshot.

The birds arrive every year in late February, having flown from as far away as Brazil. They get busy carrying pine needles, mud, and threads of oak tree moss into the birdhouse to build their nests to prepare for a new generation.

A few days into July, after they've hatched a new brood of fledgling young, the purple martins are gone, headed back to South America. Disappointed, I try to adjust to their absence. Doubt and fear creep in and grow. *What if the martins don't return? What if the lab test results are not good? What if my professor rejects my work?*

The fear lingers in church the next day, distracting me from the sermon. I look up at the large wooden cross nailed on the wall behind the altar as the minister points to it and asks, "Do you know that fear died upon the cross?"

In that moment, Jesus replaces my fear with a faith that assures me whatever happens, I will be okay. And, yes, the purple martins will return.
—MELODY BONNETTE SWANG

Lord, Your natural world is full of lessons in faith.
Thank You for giving me one right in my own backyard.

Write your fears on a scrap of paper. Then rip them into shreds to distract you no more from God's faith-filled blessings.

ALWAYS PRESENT

"And remember, I am with you always...." —MATTHEW 28:20 (NRSV)

LIKE MANY FIVE-YEAR-OLDS, FRANCES IS AFRAID OF THE DARK. SHE WANTS her blinds left open, her door ajar, and a light on. Even so, she dreads going to bed. "I don't want to close my eyes, Daddy." She crawled into bed and clutched her blanket. Her lip quivered.

I groped for something to say. What I wanted to communicate to Frances was that with God watching over her there was nothing to fear. But that was such an abstract idea.

Suddenly, I thought of the fun time we'd had after dinner, listening to some music. At one point I'd looked over at the kitchen table and watched Frances bent industriously over her coloring book. She looked up at me and smiled. "I love this song, Daddy," she said. "It makes me happy."

Sitting on the edge of her bed, I reached over and stroked her hair. "Remember when we were in the kitchen and Mom and I were doing the dishes while you and Benji played?" I asked. She nodded. "That was fun, right?" She nodded again. "Well, that was God's love we were all feeling. And that love is right here in this room with you now. It never goes away."

Frances made her concentrating face. She didn't say anything, but I could tell my words were connecting. "You think you can close your eyes and try to sleep now?" She nodded. I bent down and kissed her forehead. She closed her eyes. "God is with you," I whispered as I stood to go. This time I knew she understood. —JIM HINCH

God, help me to see You in all things.

 Remember a poem that makes you happy. Recite your favorite verse.

STOP, PRAY, LISTEN

"Be careful, keep calm and don't be afraid. Do not lose heart...."
—ISAIAH 7:4 (NIV)

IN MY 130-GALLON AQUARIUM IS A SCHOOL OF LARGE, ROUND, FLAT FISH called red hooks. They get their name from a red fin that curves like a hook. Highly nervous creatures, they react to unfamiliar noises or movement with a mad dash to the other end of the tank.

One of them is a "poster fish" for making things worse than they need to be: Leaping Larry, I call him. When Larry is startled, he jumps out of the tank. While the others are swimming back to normal, there's Larry, flopping on the carpet. You'd think he'd learn, but the next time a strange shadow crosses the tank, Larry's over the edge again.

I can't be too hard on Larry because I also tend to jump out of panic. Years ago, when my husband, Whitney, was laid off from work, I jumped into a low-paying job I hated, punishing both myself and my family. If I'd stopped, prayed, and listened, I might have heard God beyond my panic, Who had a better provision for us.

I've jumped into other things out of fear too: volunteering when I don't have time; exhausting myself with cleaning at the news of last-minute company; leaving multiple phone messages for a daughter who hasn't called when I thought she should. Fear can run my life, if I let it. The key for me is to stop, pray, listen to God. He is always ready to help me get back in the tank.
—SHARI SMYTH

Lord, when fear knocks, help me to keep still and let You answer.

When fear threatens to make you a "Leaping Larry," be still and know that He is God.

COURAGE IN THE FACE OF FEAR

Fear thou not; for I am with thee: be not dismayed; for I am thy God: I will strengthen thee; yea, I will help thee; yea, I will uphold thee with the right hand of my righteousness. —ISAIAH 41:10 (KJV)

SITTING ACROSS THE TABLE FROM MY FATHER, I STARE AT HIM. *YOU HAVE always oozed such confidence*, I think admiringly. When I was a child, my father was always present, always providing, always reaching for the stars. I wanted to be just like him. Now, this silver-haired, eighty-two-year-old man with a pacemaker and an oxygen compressor as constant companions is still trying new things, like completing educational requirements to become a mediator.

"You never seem afraid," I say to him. "I wish I had your confidence."

"I was afraid sometimes," he replies, and I am startled. This is a side of my father I've never known. He's never once discussed his fears.

"Like when?"

"When I first went to work at the Pentagon," he says. My mouth drops open. My memories of him going to work are images of a confident man in a suit and tie, his ubiquitous cowboy boots clicking down the sidewalk. "The Pentagon was so big," he continues. "There was so much responsibility."

I think of things that have frightened me: raising a daughter and son alone; eventually leaving my own government job for a new career. I smile and reach across the table to touch my father's hand. This revelation that he has wrangled with fear is a wonderful gift. —SHARON FOSTER

Lord, thank You for a father who set a fine example of courage in the face of fear. Indeed, You were courageous even unto death.

Ask an aging loved one about their younger years. If they reveal areas of vulnerability, thank them for their courageous legacy.

COMFORT THROUGH THE STORMS

Jesus spoke to them and said, "Take heart, it is I; do not be afraid."
—MATTHEW 14:27 (NRSV)

I WAS CLEANING UP THE DEBRIS FROM HURRICANE GUSTAV. ALTHOUGH I'd breathed a sigh of relief, it wasn't over yet. Hurricane Hannah had turned toward the East Coast, but Ike was on its way into the Gulf and Josephine wasn't far behind.

Lord, I prayed silently as I picked up broken branches, *watch over us. I'm afraid.* As my brief prayer ended, I heard voices coming from the tennis courts across from my backyard pond.

Two women were playing. As they hit the ball back and forth, one called out, "God always sees us through."

"Yes," her partner called back, "we just have to let go of our fear and latch on to our faith."

What a perfect message for me today, I thought.

The next morning in church, I listened to the story of Jesus calming His disciples on the stormy Sea of Galilee. "Do not be afraid," Jesus had said.

That afternoon I walked outside and gazed across the pond. My fear was gone. —MELODY BONNETTE SWANG

Father, thank You for the words that comfort me
through the storms in my life.

Meditate on the words of the old hymn, "Master, the Tempest Is Raging": "The winds and the waves shall obey Thy will. Peace, be still!"

UNAFRAID

The Spirit you received does not make you slaves, so that you live in fear again.
—ROMANS 8:15 (NIV)

THE HOTEL TERRACE OVERLOOKED A SLOPING FIELD SURROUNDED BY A WIRE fence. From where I sat with my coffee, I could see, inside the enclosure, a grazing doe and, prancing by her side, a spotted fawn.

Finding his mother indifferent to his capering, the fawn began experimenting with various paces: galloping, bucking, leaping. Now a mincing little dance, lifting each hoof daintily one by one, and then a stiff-legged march, first right legs, then left. 'Round and 'round the circumference of the fence he trotted, savoring the newfound delights of four legs, while my coffee grew cold, forgotten.

Suddenly the fawn whirled to face the wire screen. On the other side was a dog about his own size—from his eager pawing at the fence, still a puppy. Both of them shivering with excitement, the two young animals stood nose to nose, tails wagging furiously.

Then the doe thundered down the slope and thrust herself between the fence and the fawn. Prodding him with her head, she drove him swiftly back up the hill. I could almost hear the lecture: *Never, never, ever go near a dog!*

The puppy whimpered; his tail drooped. The fawn stood subdued. But I felt as though for a wondrous moment I'd been given a glimpse of Eden, before the first fear entered the world. Some fears are realistic, of course, on this post-Eden planet. Dogs, the doe knew, kill deer. But what if I could be, most of the time, as trusting and adventurous and full of joy as that fawn? —ELIZABETH SHERRILL

Teach me, Father, to distinguish needful fears from the false ones
that block full enjoyment of Your world.

 Invest some time in nature today. Then journal about your discoveries.

EMBRACED BY LOVE

"Surely God is my salvation; I will trust and not be afraid...." —ISAIAH 12:2 (NIV)

I SAT NERVOUSLY IN THE WAITING ROOM OF THE HOSPITAL LAB, READING A book to six-year-old Solomon and two-year-old Henry. When Henry's name was called for his blood test, my husband, Tony, picked him up and disappeared behind the door. In moments Henry's cries filled the room.

Solomon and I tried to read the next page of our book. From behind the door, Henry's screams escalated to panicked shrieks.

I reached for Solomon's hand. "It's okay," I said.

"I know," Solomon said. "Henry just doesn't understand."

I nodded. "You're right," I said. "He needs to have this done."

"Dad is with him, right?" Solomon asked.

"Yes."

Henry's cries continued. Finally my husband came out with a tear-streaked Henry, who looked down at the small trinket he held in his hands.

Tony nodded and said, "He even got to pick a toy from the treasure chest."

In the car Solomon reached his hand over to Henry's and held it. "It's okay, Henry," he said. "We love you. We were right there, Dad with you and Mom with me right outside the door." Henry smiled.

That night, I thought about the day and my own struggles. So often I find myself crying over a situation that I just don't understand, an experience that will ultimately make me better, wiser, more understanding. Just like Henry, I'm not alone and I'm always embraced with love. —SABRA CIANCANELLI

Father, thank You for always being there.

> Has there been a time recently when God has been "right there" for you? Share your proven path with a treasured friend over coffee.

COURAGE TO FACE TOMORROW

"Be strong and courageous. Do not be afraid; do not be discouraged, for the Lord your God will be with you wherever you go." —Joshua 1:9 (NIV)

Tomorrow I'm going in for one of my regular cancer tests, and today I'm fighting my "What if" fears.

What if my cancer comes back?

Nearly seven years ago I was diagnosed with stage IV ovarian cancer and I was given a two-year life expectancy. I've beaten all odds. But a couple of doctors said, "Stage IV ovarian cancer always comes back." So far I've proven them wrong, but before every checkup the "What if" fears start creeping in.

What if my test is not good?

"Don't go there," a friend advises me. But I have to go there. My way of dealing with my fears is to look the worst-case possibilities square in the face. I've even created my own scenario. I imagine my fears stuffed into an imaginary room. It's a scary but sacred place, because nothing in that room surprises God—and He invites me to "go there" because Jesus is there too. He walks alongside me as I explore each fear, imagining if that worst possibility became a reality.

What if my cancer comes back?

I picture Jesus answering, "If your cancer comes back, I will still be with you. I will still give you what you need. I will still love you with an everlasting love. And I will still give you a future with hope."

Soon, I know that even if my worst fears become reality, Jesus's promises are still true. That gives me courage. —Carol Kuykendall

Lord, Your promises sustain me. Always.

> Replace the "What If" fears in your life with "What Is" truths: God is love. God never changes. God will never leave me or forsake me.

CALLING ON JESUS

"Get up, pick up your pallet and walk." —JOHN 5:8 (NAS)

I HAVE THIS THEORY: I THINK MOST OF US STRUGGLE WITH AT LEAST ONE big thing in life. For me, it's fear. Fear trips me up over and over. It's weird. If I allow even one pip-squeak of fear to tiptoe through my thoughts, it stirs up others.

What if my mind goes blank when I'm speaking in front of a crowd of people?
What if this mole isn't just a mole?
What if...? What if...? What if...?

Fear has been my enemy for as long as I can remember. When I'm really honest with myself, I have to admit that it feels more natural to worry and be afraid. Maybe I get charged on the energy. Who knows?

Sometimes—many times—I'll write in my prayer journal, "Jesus, I know I must be wearing You out with this same old, same old." And I sense Him smiling at me, laughing in a kind, relaxed sort of way. As I read these words from John 5:8, I can almost hear Him say: "Get up, pick up your pallet, and walk, Julie. You don't have to stay in fear, all huddled under the sheets today. You've been stuck here on your pallet before, remember? Get up, girl. Get out of that sickbed. You have a life to live. There's freedom, if you want it."

When I choose to take Jesus's hand and let Him lead me, the fear scrams. Every single time. —JULIE GARMON

Lord, I'm reaching for Your hand today. Let's dance again.

Is there something *you* return to again and again? Jealousy, perhaps, or anger? Visualize it at the foot of the cross, and leave it there.

HEROIC FAITH

"You're blessed when you can show people how to cooperate.... That's when you discover who you really are, and your place in God's family." —MATTHEW 5:9 (MSG)

WHEN STATEWIDE INOCULATIONS STARTED IN OKLAHOMA DURING THE Depression, my first-grade class was one of the first to be given shots. My mother came to school that day to help the teacher and the nurse calm us.

When the first girl got her shot, she screamed and then sobbed. Many of the other children started crying too. I slipped toward the back of the room, hoping they would run out before I got up there.

I saw my mother talking to the teacher and the nurse. Then she walked briskly toward me and whispered, "Keith, everyone is afraid. It would help so much if you would go up there and say you want to get your shot now. It only hurts a little. You can do it."

It was the last thing I wanted to do. I didn't care how the other kids felt; I felt terrible. But I had to do it. So I calmly walked to the nurse, looked her in the eye, rolled up my sleeve, and said, "I'll go next." Somehow I managed not to cry or scream. Then I rolled my sleeve down and calmly walked back to my desk.

I learned something that day: Maybe the heroes my mother had read to me about were sometimes afraid. *Even courageous people have fear*, I thought. —KEITH MILLER

Lord, thank You that even though You asked three times to
be excused on Gethsemane, You went ahead anyway.
Give me the courage to love enough to follow
You wherever Your adventure leads me.

What challenges are you facing today? Take one bold step toward meeting it.

BOUNDLESS GRACE

"My grace is sufficient for you, for my power is made perfect in weakness."
—2 CORINTHIANS 12:9 (NIV)

YESTERDAY MORNING, AS I TOOK COFFEE ON THE DECK, A CHARTREUSE glimmer caught my eye. A tiny inchworm dropped out of the air, paused, then dropped some more to hang in space with no visible support. A breeze revealed its suspension thread when it swayed and flashed silver. This inchworm hung about ten feet off the ground and about twenty feet below the nearest maple branch. It remained still for only a few minutes, then began to hump and stretch, and hump and stretch, literally inching up its lifeline as insubstantial as a hair. I sat hypnotized by the determination and trust of this speck of life.

I can relate to its precarious existence.

About a year ago, I gave up my apartment, stashed my furniture and other belongings in my daughter's basement, and embarked upon my Year of Houseless Living, the better to afford international travel and writing retreats. By renting rooms, house- and pet-sitting, staying with relatives and friends, I have enjoyed shelter, companionship, and productive creativity. Though I calculate that I have slept in twenty-five beds, not once have I feared that I would have no shelter. Why, just this week, more monthlong house-sitting invitations—and new creative ideas to pursue—have come my way!

Though to the casual observer both the inchworm and I may appear to live high-risk, insecure lives, we know better. God's boundless grace supports us every moment. —GAIL THORELL SCHILLING

Lord of all grace, how You amaze me!

Take your coffee or tea break near a window or outside and consider God's "next step" for you.

GOOD NEWS

And the angel said unto them, Fear not: for, behold, I bring you good tidings of great joy.... —LUKE 2:10 (KJV)

"I WANT THE DOCTOR TO LOOK AT THESE PICTURES," THE SONOGRAM technician said as she left the room. I lay shivering on a gurney, half-clothed, fighting off fear. I already knew I had a lump in the breast tissue under my left arm. A mammogram the week before couldn't get to the exact spot.

The only difference between now and five minutes from now will be what I know, I thought. *My body will be the same.* It was weird to think that if I had cancer, malignant cells were silently multiplying. It was weirder to realize that my day would change because of my knowledge of the disease.

With Christmas so close, I wondered if what I'd learn would ruin my holiday. In one sense, yes; in another sense, not at all. Jesus Christ was still God, born for our salvation. Christmas itself would be the same.

The door opened, and the doctor strode in. "Show me where the lump is," she said briskly. With some difficulty, I found the spot. She squirted goo onto the sonogram probe and smeared it around my underarm. "Huh," she said, "I don't see a thing."

"How can that be?" I asked. "I felt it and my doctor felt it."

"Oh, cysts come and go," she replied casually. "Yours is gone."

—JULIA ATTAWAY

Lord, whether I face happy or sad news this Christmas,
help me focus on the good news that You've given us.

❋ Think of a time when God brought you or your family unexpected good news. Live in the expectancy that He can do it again.

GRAB HOLD OF THE GOOD NEWS

The thief comes only to steal and kill and destroy.... —JOHN 10:10 (RSV)

"SUMMER 1944. SOMEWHERE IN NORTH AFRICA." THAT'S ALL THE DETAILS my letters home were allowed to provide, that third year of the war. In fact, we enlisted men didn't have much more information ourselves, other than that we'd been waiting for weeks here in this dry, hot staging area. The camp was a replacement depot, and what we'd be replacing was dead and injured soldiers.

There was one unofficial source of news. "Evening, fellows," said the sultry voice over the radio. "This is Midge at the Mike, calling from Radio Berlin. I'll be bringing you some Glenn Miller to remind you of home. Don't you wish you could go dancing tonight instead of fighting a losing war?"

Axis Sally we called her, an American girl living in Germany. How in the world did she get her information? She said we'd come over on a Cunard Line troopship (that was true) and that we would soon join the 141st Infantry Regiment in Italy (which also proved to be true). "Most of you will get killed," she said. "Too bad."

We tried to laugh, but I lay sweating on my canvas cot, scared.

Today, as I approach my eighty-eighth birthday, bad news is still broadcast over the airwaves: fearful stories of wars, natural disasters, economic downturns. This is when it's helpful to remember Axis Sally. The facts may be accurate. But when I let myself focus on these things, I'm rendered fearful and ineffective. It's how the spiritual enemy works. Why not listen instead to the Good News, which empowers us to reach out with hope to a hurting world? —JOHN SHERRILL

Father, help me hear Your voice today above
the clamor of bad news reports.

 Today, turn off the TV and listen instead to that still, small Voice.

HAVE A LITTLE FAITH

"And now, when shall I also provide for my own house?" —GENESIS 30:30 (NKJV)

I SAVED FOR RETIREMENT FROM THE TIME I WAS IN MY TWENTIES, AND AS my husband, Keith, neared the end of his career, I felt confident that we had a good nest egg. Then the economy crashed, our savings dropped more than 60 percent, a consulting gig fell away, and the publisher of my new book declared bankruptcy.

Because I've always had fears of penury, I started counting every cent, which drove Keith crazy. "We're not starving," he said. "Relax. Things will turn around."

"I don't see how," I replied.

"Have a little faith," he told me. We would find a way.

Somehow, we did—and we continue to even today. —RHODA BLECKER

Help me learn to be like my husband, Lord. He understands
Your ways so much more completely than I do.

 Take a drive out in the country. When you see the rolling landscape, remember that the One Who owns the cattle on a thousand hills will surely provide for *you.*

HELD FIRM

And now, behold, we are in thine hand.... —Joshua 9:25 (KJV)

"Take your time, ma'am," the EMT urged. "No need to rush. She's in good hands." Even though my ninety-three-year-old mother writhed in pain on the gurney, as he rolled her toward the ambulance, I knew he was right.

After a dozen wee-hour episodes like this, I also knew the routine: Call my brother, dress, find my purse and keys, and grab my knitting. I had arrived from Europe the day before, so I was jet-lagged and my hope was at low ebb.

My friends thought I was crazy to cut my sabbatical short and leave France early. Yesterday, Mom glowed with frail health and happiness. Now, she was deathly ill.

In the emergency room, Mom woke from her medication-induced peace, blinked, and clutched one of my hands. For several hours, all I could do was balance on a stool and hold that dearly familiar hand, now so thin. Was this why I felt compelled to return home to hold Mom's hand? What divine hand guided *me*? Mom had lived alone for ten years, yet tonight she hadn't remembered to push her Medic Alert button. I had done that.

Instead of knitting tonight, I hold Mom's hand—and God holds mine.
—Gail Thorell Schilling

> *Lord, You hold me gently, securely, in Your almighty palm.*
> *I have no fear.*

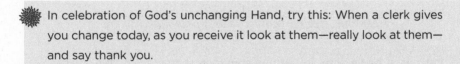
In celebration of God's unchanging Hand, try this: When a clerk gives you change today, as you receive it look at them—really look at them—and say thank you.

THE PEACEMAKER

Ye have heard that it hath been said, An eye for an eye, and a tooth for a tooth: but I say unto you, That ye resist not evil: but whosoever shall smite thee on thy right cheek, turn to him the other also. —Matthew 5:38–39 (KJV)

I HAVE BEEN WITNESSING A LOT OF ARGUMENTS LATELY—ON THE STREETS, in cars, even between friends—and I find myself frozen, unsure of what to do. Then, the other day, I suddenly remembered an incident from my childhood.

The playground in elementary school was a safe and fun place, but by junior high, relationships between boys had become more complicated and dangerous. Just as my memories of elementary days usually center on sunshine and climbing on the jungle gym, my memories of junior high are equally dark. There were fights almost every day.

The violence of other boys scared me. I knew that a Christian was supposed to be different, but I had no idea how to accomplish anything but fear.

One afternoon when school was over, two boys began to argue and push each other. I was standing next to a friend of mine who was also a Christian. I thought that he, too, was frightened. And maybe he was, but he surprised me by what he did. Just as the boys went from pushing to punching each other, my friend ran to them. "Don't! Don't! Don't!" he yelled, hiding his face as he waved his arms in front of them. The commotion that my friend caused made the boys stop. One of them ran away. The other began to cry. It was the most courageous act that I ever saw. —Jon Sweeney

Holy One, give me courage to be a peacemaker today.

Let peace begin with you. When someone shares a juicy bit of news with you today, counter it with something authentically good you can say about the one they are hurting.

MAKING ROOM FOR PEACE

When my spirit was overwhelmed within me, then You knew my path....
—PSALM 142:3 (NKJV)

ON HER EIGHTH BIRTHDAY, MY NEIGHBOR GIRL WITH SPECIAL NEEDS invited me to her family's celebration: cake, soda, and balloons. Five adults gathered around the table, sang the traditional song, and urged her to blow out the candles. She stared, silent as breath. Her mother, grandmother, and I modeled technique, blowing out one candle at a time. She laughed when her grandmother ran a finger through the icing and marked her cheek. Still, the girl watched the burning candles, speechless, until finally an adult blew out the last flame. After lots of clapping, everyone ate cake. A nice little party.

Or so I thought. Fifteen minutes later, she and I sat out on our shared front stoop. "That was a great birthday, wasn't it?"

"Yes," she stammered, "but I didn't get to blow out my candles."

"Were you afraid?" I asked.

"Yes. Too many people."

"Well, let's try again," I suggested.

Days later, I felt unnerved; the week's demands overwhelmed me. When I heard the school bus brakes and watched my friend trudge into her day, I remembered our workable solution to her birthday dilemma. Identify the problem and bring a fearsome obstacle down to a manageable size. As I scaled back my to-do list, I made room for God's peace. —EVELYN BENCE

Lord, when my loved ones and I feel overwhelmed, help me see
options that point us away from fear and toward peace.

 Make a list of what you will do when a problem overwhelms you.

COMING THROUGH THE STORM

Consider it pure joy, my brothers and sisters, whenever you face trials of many kinds.
—JAMES 1:2 (NIV)

AFTER A BAD STORM UNEXPECTEDLY BLEW THROUGH MANDEVILLE, LOUISIANA, I went outside to survey the neighborhood.

"Looks like a small twister went through here!" I called out to my neighbor, who was walking her dog.

"Sure looks like it," she said. "How'd you make out?"

"Awful!" I said. "The wind ripped off some siding from the back of the house and put some deep scratches into the bedroom windows. A bunch of fencing is down in the backyard, and my purple martin birdhouse is knocked down. It's just terrible." I sighed, shaking my head. "How'd you do?"

"A big tree fell through my roof and crashed into my kitchen," she said. "I've got lots of water and structural damage."

"Oh no," I said. "I'm so sorry."

"It's okay," she said. "I've been praying about whether or not to remodel my kitchen." She smiled. "Looks like I got my answer."

"Wow," I said. "You sure have a great attitude about it."

"I'm keeping in mind the quote that I hung in my kitchen: 'I got this one, okay? Love, God.'"

She tugged at her dog's leash to coax him on. "Thank goodness that quote survived the storm. We will too." —MELODY BONNETTE SWANG

Next time, God, I want to respond to calamity with
a graciousness that reflects my faith in You.

 Find and frame a faith-filled quote to hang in your own kitchen.

FACING YOUR GREATEST FEAR

Walk in the ways of thine heart, and in the sight of thine eyes....
—ECCLESIASTES 11:9 (KJV)

MY FIRST THOUGHT WHEN THE NEW MOON-SHAPED SHADOW OBSCURED the vision above my left eye was *Oh, it must be these new glasses!* But when I took them off, the shadow remained.

As he shined a piercing white light into my dilated eye, my ophthalmologist said, "It's probably just a floater."

A week later my left eye could see only fuzzy shapes through a dull gray curtain. This time when the doctor examined my eye, he said, "You have a hole in the macula" (the part of the eye that sees). He sent me to a surgeon who discovered a detached retina and told his assistant to give me his first available surgical appointment.

My husband, Robert, held my hand as we walked back to the car, tears sliding down my face onto my shirt. It wasn't the surgery I feared; it was the possible loss of sight. The diagnosis of macular degeneration in my right eye had been on my chart for three years. But this was my left eye! I remembered Dr. Bode's words: "It may not happen for a long time, but if you live long enough..."

Well, this is it. I must have lived long enough for my left eye to become affected!
Seeing has always been one of my most valued gifts, and blindness my greatest fear. Now it was happening. —MARILYN MORGAN KING

Creator God, it seems the time has come.
Please lead me through the dark.

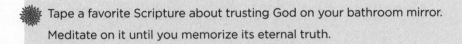
Tape a favorite Scripture about trusting God on your bathroom mirror. Meditate on it until you memorize its eternal truth.

LOOK TO THE FATHER

For I am the Lord your God who takes hold of your right hand and says to you, Do not fear; I will help you. —ISAIAH 41:13 (NIV)

MY FRIEND LINDA NEEDED TO TALK, SO WE WALKED OVER TO THE PARK. "Business is slow, and I'm considering returning to school to finish my degree," she confided. "I'm afraid though. I believe it's God's plan for me, but I can't seem to move forward. God has always been there for me. Yet…" Her voice trailed off.

"Let's pray about it, okay?" I offered.

We sat in silence for a moment and then both looked over in the direction of the playground. A father was coaxing his little girl down the slide—she at the top, clutching the rail, and he at the bottom, his arms outstretched.

"Honey," he said, "I'm right here."

"I'm scared," she replied.

"But, honey," he said gently, "have I ever let you fall?"

She shook her head.

"Then give it a try, okay?" he asked.

"Okay," she said reluctantly. With that, she let go and slid into his arms.

"Daddy, that was fun!" she exclaimed. "Let's do it again!"

Linda looked over at me with a big smile. "Looks like I just got a perfect lesson in faith," she said, laughing. "Okay, Lord, here I come! Just make sure You catch me, okay?" —MELODY BONNETTE SWANG

Father, help me to let go of the fear in my life that stops me from following You. Amen.

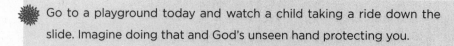 Go to a playground today and watch a child taking a ride down the slide. Imagine doing that and God's unseen hand protecting you.

Thank You for being the storm over me, Lord. I cried out in despair, but I never knew it was You, washing things and making them new.

....

KAREN VALENTIN

Chapter 4

WHEN YOU FEEL ANXIOUS

....

Let's take Jesus at His word. When He says we're forgiven, let's unload the guilt. When He says we're valuable, let's believe Him. When He says we're eternal, let's bury our fear. When He says we're provided for, let's stop worrying.

MAX LUCADO

ONE DAY AT A TIME

"Therefore I say to you, do not worry about your life, what you will eat or what you will drink; nor about your body, what you will put on...." —MATTHEW 6:25 (NKJV)

HOW CAN YOU SAY THAT, LORD? DON'T YOU KNOW HOW COSTLY THINGS ARE?

"Is not life more than food and the body more than clothing?"

Well, yes, but we can't go around naked and eating crackers all day.

"Look at the birds! They don't plant or harvest, but they aren't hungry."

Okay, but birds don't have to drive a car or make quarterly income tax payments.

"Look at the lilies in the fields; they don't work nine-to-five, and yet Solomon himself was not so well-clad."

But flowers only live a few days. I might live seventy, eighty, ninety years; that's a lot of house payments and car payments and prescription drugs.

"But you are more important to Me than birds and flowers. I know you need all these things. There is nothing I don't understand."

But my wife has always wanted to go to England, and I would like to retire.

"I never promised you that all your dreams would come true in this life, or that you would have everything your neighbors have. But if you will put Me first, everything you really need will be taken care of."

I don't like surprises, God. I want to know where my next meal is coming from.

"Life is full of surprises, but just take it one day at a time."

—DANIEL SCHANTZ

> *My faith is small, Lord, about the size of a mustard seed.*
> *But You said that's enough to move mountains,*
> *so I'm trusting You to care for me.*

Write two columns of your wants vs. needs. Place the paper in your Bible where Matthew 6:25 is. Refer to it often.

LEAVE THE OUTCOME TO GOD

For we are God's handiwork, created in Christ Jesus to do good works, which God prepared in advance for us to do. —EPHESIANS 2:10 (NIV)

IT'S HARD TO IMAGINE A WORSE ENVIRONMENT FOR GIVING A MOTIVATIONAL speech.

I was standing between the tables in the center of a hospital cafeteria between the entrance and the food itself, which meant a steady stream of people stepped around me as I spoke. There had been no advance publicity for my speech, so the audience was made up of the usual patrons of the cafeteria. I didn't have a microphone to help my voice compete with the giant flat-screen television, and a baby was screaming about ten feet away from me.

In the middle of all this, I was attempting to give a talk about my battle with cancer and the loss of my leg. I took a deep breath and remembered what my mother had told me before the presentation. "Even if it seems like a tough room to give a speech in, maybe you'll be able to touch just one person."

Doubtful, I thought.

After I finished, there was a smattering of applause. I was eager to leave, but as I did, a young man grabbed my shoulder.

"I lost both my legs in the war," he said, gesturing down toward his two prosthetic limbs. "I really appreciate you sharing your story today."
—JOSHUA SUNDQUIST

Lord, please give me the patience I need to do my work and leave the outcome to You.

The next time you have to address a group, tell yourself it's more than enough to reach an audience of one.

GOD WILL TAKE CARE OF YOU

He provides food for those who fear him; he remembers his covenant forever.
—Psalm 111:5 (NIV)

As a gymnastics coach I'm constantly lifting mats, moving equipment, and helping children as they swing, climb, and somersault through the air. When my husband and I found out I was pregnant, I asked the doctor about the potential dangers at work. "You don't have to worry right now," she'd said, "but the bigger you get, the more risk you'll have for back problems."

I considered leaving work after my fifth month of pregnancy, but money was a concern. "We'll be fine," my husband said, but I had doubts.

At a weekly Bible study, I explained my situation as we all shared prayer requests. "I've never had to depend on someone else to take care of me," I admitted. "What if it's not enough?"

Aliza, an older woman, smiled at me and shook her head. She held my hands. "You can't depend on yourself or your husband. God will take care of your family, and it will always be enough."

After her encouraging words, I made a decision to leave after the fall semester. I didn't know how everything would work out, but I knew I could trust in the One Who had always taken care of me.

Just weeks after I gave my notice. A company interested in some of my work attracted me. They wanted to give me a contract at three times my rate!

It was more than enough. I thanked the Lord, not just for the financial blessing but for confirming Aliza's words so quickly. —Karen Valentin

Lord, You are my provider. You have always taken care of me,
and it will always be enough.

 God is your first resort, not your last. Praise Him for His provision.

EXHALE YOUR FRUSTRATIONS

Place these words on your hearts. Get them deep inside you....
—DEUTERONOMY 11:18 (MSG)

LAST NIGHT I HAD TROUBLE SLEEPING, WHICH IS RARE FOR A WOMAN WHO has been nicknamed "the log" by her husband. Perry has always lived by this remedy for occasional insomnia: First, stay in bed. "Even if you aren't sleeping, your body can rest." Second, while you lie there, recite Bible verses.

For the past week, I'd been reading a handful of psalms over and over again, until I'd allowed those divine words to read me. So as I lay there not-sleeping, I decided to try Perry's methods. I folded my hands across my chest, let my heavy eyelids fall shut, exhaled my frustrations over my wakefulness, and whispered the poetic fragments God had written on my heart:

For you created my inmost being; you knit me together in my mother's womb. I praise you because I am fearfully and wonderfully made.

Blessed is the man who does not walk in the counsel of the wicked or stand in the way of sinners or sit in the seat of mockers.... He is like a tree planted by streams of water.

Even in darkness, light dawns for the upright, for the gracious, compassionate, righteous man.

Within minutes of murmuring those passages, I had drifted off to sleep. Truth is the most comfortable of pillows for the body, the mind, the soul.
—ASHLEY WIERSMA

Father, thank You for the unparalleled restfulness
I find in Your timelessly tranquil Word.

Instead of counting sheep when sleep eludes you, count the times your Heavenly Father has been there for you in the past week.

GO TO GOD FIRST

By the sadness of the countenance the heart is made better. —ECCLESIASTES 7:3 (KJV)

IN MY LATER FORTIES I FIRST NOTICED THE LOSSES OF MIDDLE AGE: THE loss of energy and looks; the empty nest; the loss of friends and dreams; problems with my feet and knees, my eyes and teeth.

I pretended these losses didn't matter, but they did. One day I went to the dentist about a problem tooth. He worked on it and then said, "I'm sorry, but I can't save this tooth."

"That's okay," I said nonchalantly, "teeth don't last forever." He extracted it; I paid the nurse and headed out the door. It was a beautiful day, and there is no greater feeling than that of leaving the dentist's office. I was whistling as I walked briskly to the car.

Suddenly, I felt moisture on my left cheek. I realized that I was crying—crying over the loss of a tooth. It was the tipping point.

I managed to make it to the car before I broke down. I sat there in the front seat, like a little boy sitting on his father's lap, seeking comfort. The loss of my tooth enabled me to extract all my other griefs and present them to God.

When at last I regained my composure, I felt a hundred pounds lighter. That cry was probably worth a year's therapy.

Now when I experience a loss, I go to God first, instead of waiting until my load is so heavy that it interferes with my happiness. —DANIEL SCHANTZ

Thank You for not leaving me, God,
when other things are going away.

In your mind's eye, climb onto your Heavenly Father's lap and tell Him about the pain in your heart. Great or small, He will understand like no other.

GOD'S ANSWER TO "WHAT IF?"

When anxiety was great within me, your consolation brought me joy.
—PSALM 94:19 (NIV)

MY WIFE, JULEE, CALLED RIGHT BEFORE 5:00 AM. SHE WAS IN THE BERKSHIRE Hills, preparing our house for a Thanksgiving family gathering. I planned to take the train up from New York City later, but everything had changed.

"I fell down the stairs," she moaned. "The paramedics are here. It looks like I broke my collarbone. I'm going to the hospital."

"I'll be there as fast as I can."

"Call someone to come over and take care of Millie. She's hysterical." Our young golden retriever had never seen a commotion like this.

I threw some things in a bag, called our friend Chrissy to check on Millie and then go to see Julee in the emergency room, and ran a few blocks to Penn Station, where I got a seat on the next train, due to leave in an hour's time.

What a long hour it was. I was too distracted even to pray. *What if Julee needs surgery? What if it's worse than just a fractured clavicle?*

"The what-ifs will drive us crazy," a friend once told me. *What if*, I reminded myself, *God is in charge? I just need to step out of the way and calm down.*

That's the what-if that mattered. Julee did break her collarbone, but she was going to be okay, and we had an interesting Thanksgiving with me doing the cooking. Millie was her joyous self once we were all reunited. *What if*, I reminded myself again a few days later as we waved good-bye to my family, *after all these years I just learn to let God take charge when I can't?* —EDWARD GRINNAN

*Father, You never fail us in times of need. Next time I'll try
to remember the most important what-if of all.*

Consider this: "What if" God loves you as if you were His only child? (He does, you know.)

ACTING WISELY

"I, wisdom, dwell together with prudence; I possess knowledge and discretion."
—PROVERBS 8:12 (NIV)

"YOU DID WHAT?" SAID MY WIFE, AGHAST AT THE NEWS I HAD GIVEN HER.
"What were you thinking?" We were on the subway—she taking Maggie,
twelve, to an art supply store; me taking Stephen, ten, on an outing to
Governors Island.

Just what was I thinking? A couple of weeks earlier, I'd offered to put up a
friend for a few days. We had no room, our daughter Elizabeth was about to
pay us a visit from college, and Maggie was having a difficult time. My offer
was impulsive; I'd wanted to help a friend, but I hadn't considered the circumstances at home when I invited him.

Now, I don't think I'm entirely lacking in common sense. My problem is the
anxiety that comes with my depression. Even a relatively small decision becomes
fraught and worrisome, and I short-circuit the worry by doing the first thing that
comes to mind. As you can imagine, that leads to a lot of bad decisions.

What am I doing about it? Working with a counselor to control my anxious thoughts and remembering to pray when I feel the anxiety coming on.
As for my friend? Forty-five minutes later I was sitting on the steps of the old
customs house in lower Manhattan with my cell phone, straightening things
out with him. —ANDREW ATTAWAY

Father, Your Spirit is peace and Your every decision is wise.
Help me to think carefully and act wisely.

Truly pray without ceasing. Consult your Heavenly Father before making any decisions today.

CHANGE IS GOOD

I will clothe thee with change.... —ZECHARIAH 3:4 (KJV)

"DAVID, I'M RUNNING BEHIND," I SAID TO MY HUSBAND. "WOULD YOU please slice the mushrooms for the salad?"

A few minutes later, our family was gathered around the kitchen table. "Mom, what are these round things in the salad?" our son Brock asked.

"Some new kind of vegetable?" our daughter Keri chimed in.

"They have a texture like mushrooms," Keri's husband, Ben, said.

I looked at the salad and laughed. "Great. I ask your dad to slice the mushrooms and he invents a totally new way to do it!" I'd never seen mushrooms cut in perfect rounds. They looked like full moons floating in a sky of greens.

Later, while I was cleaning the dishes, a rush of apprehension swept across my heart. David was retiring as pastor of Hillsboro Presbyterian Church after thirty-seven years. We were so young when we came, and it had been our life for so long; now our future was uncertain.

I saw a circle of mushroom clinging to a plate. "I'm like you," I whispered. "My life is taking a completely new shape. I have no idea who I'll become."

David reappeared from the porch, where he'd been saying good-bye to the kids. "Guess I flunked Mushroom Cutting 101," he said.

"*Hmm*, I don't know," I answered, holding that last mushroom moon up to the light. "Maybe change is good. It's actually kind of pretty, don't you think?" —PAM KIDD

Father, a transition is coming.
Reshape me as You would have me be.

List five major changes you've experienced in your life. Reflect on how God led you through each one.

LIVING OUR DREAMS

"Remember, Lord, how I have walked before you faithfully and with wholehearted devotion and have done what is good in your eyes." —ISAIAH 38:3 (NIV)

MY DREAM HAD COME TRUE. AFTER MONTHS OF UNEMPLOYMENT AND A move to a new state, I landed the perfect job: I was going to work at a bakery.

Baking has long been a passion of mine. I'd longed to find a bakery in our new hometown that would allow me to work part-time, so I could keep up with my freelance work and get to know the people in my community.

Finally I'd found a bakery I loved and landed an interview. Now I had an e-mail in my in-box, asking when I could start.

But I fretted. *Is it enough money? What if I do a terrible job and get fired?*

As I spiraled down the staircase of self-doubt, my husband, Brian, interjected, "You want to do this, right?"

"Of course!" I replied.

"Then do it," he said. "Run the numbers, evaluate your options, and then do it. Have a little faith."

His last comment was made in passing, but it really struck me. We were miles from our old hometown in a new city we'd trusted God to bring us to. And He'd provided my husband with an amazing career opportunity and me with not merely a job, but my dream job. And I was fretting and doubting.

I took a deep breath, said a prayer, and accepted the offer. Sure, I've messed up a few transactions and needed help filling certain orders, but I've learned to do the job. And to stop worrying and trust God. —ASHLEY KAPPEL

Lord, thank You for allowing me to live my dream.

For decisions large and small, reflect on this simple prayer: "In Thee, O Lord, do I put my trust."

CHANGING AN ANXIOUS HEART

Then shalt thou call, and the Lord shall answer; thou shalt cry, and he shall say,
Here I am.... —ISAIAH 58:9 (KJV)

YESTERDAY I STOOD IN A SHOPPING MALL DRESSING ROOM, FORCING MYSELF
to try on bathing suits to replace my dilapidated tank suit. How had my
once-girlish figure gone from lithesome to lumbering so fast?

Trying to wriggle out of a spandex suit for a "mature figure," I bounced
against the wall. Someone in the next dressing room asked if I was okay. *No!*
I wanted to yell. *I'm older, heavier, and way more insecure than I ever thought I'd be.*

I left the store without buying anything, feeling upset. Then, as I looked at
the sun glinting off a balloon soaring above me, I consulted God.

"I'm older," a woeful voice said.

Another voice answered right back, *Yup, you are.*

"I don't know what the future will bring."

Nobody does.

"My health could fail."

It might.

"I can't stand to live with this anxiety."

Don't have to.

"But I'm stuck! I'll always be inadequate and anxious!"

No, you won't. You can change. You can accept that life changes and trust that
I'll always be present to help you. —MARY ANN O'ROARK

> *Dear God, help me to be aware that You're always "talking back to me."*
> *And help me actually to listen.*

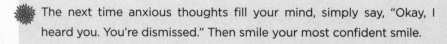 The next time anxious thoughts fill your mind, simply say, "Okay, I
heard you. You're dismissed." Then smile your most confident smile.

GOD'S GIFT OF LAUGHTER

There is an appointed time for everything…a time to weep and a time to laugh.…
—ECCLESIASTES 3:1, 4 (NAS)

I THOUGHT I WAS MAKING REAL PROGRESS IN MY PATH TOWARD A SIMPLER life when the unexpected happened: My laundry room and walk-in closet flooded, thanks to century-old pipes. In a panic, I lugged my best clothes upstairs to a clear spot in the living room. Over in a corner were more clothes, brought from my parents' home to sort for a charitable donation.

"Ask for help when you need it," I'd recently read in a book on decluttering. Desperate, I telephoned James, who'd rescued a friend from several household disasters. "Don't you worry, ma'am," he told me. "We'll get 'er done."

By eleven o'clock, James was knocking on the front door of the cabin. I ushered him into the living room, although not much living had been done there of late. "Excuse the mess," I began. "But I guess that's why you're here."

James gazed wide-eyed from one end of the living room to the other. The space was jam-packed with clothes; you could hardly see the glistening log walls with their gray mortar chinking. I was filled with shame that I'd allowed my cabin, the one spot on earth that was mine alone, to fall into such a state. Then James piped up: "Got any thirty-six thirty-two blue jeans?"

Oh no! James thinks my home is a store! I began to laugh.

My father's pants were precisely what James had in mind. "Let's get to work and see what we can find," I said. —ROBERTA MESSNER

Thank You, God, for helpers who come to my rescue—with humor.

Is there someone who has helped you with an important task? Ask them to meet you for an ice-cream cone and find something to chuckle about.

TRUSTING GOD'S PROTECTION

Thou shalt not be afraid for the terror by night; nor for the arrow that flieth by day; nor for the pestilence that walketh in darkness; nor for the destruction that wasteth at noonday. —Psalm 91:5–6 (KJV)

I'm a bit of a germaphobe, especially during flu season, when every cough and sneeze makes me cringe. So imagine my discomfort the other day when I was stuck on a crowded commuter train and the man in front of me went into a coughing fit. He would cough violently for a few minutes and then it would subside, only to resume as soon as I thought I could start breathing again.

God, I prayed miserably, *please make him stop. I can't afford to get sick.*

But this man wasn't stopping. I scrunched lower in my seat, imagining a thick cloud of airborne pathogens was filling the car. Anger and anxiety roiled within me as I watched the seat back in front of me buck with every cough. Suddenly, the young woman across the aisle pulled out a bottle of water from her bag, and handed it to the man. "Here you go," she said. "Might help."

The man took a sip, and another, clearing his throat. "Must have had something stuck," he said to the woman. "Thanks."

"You can keep it," she said with a smile, nodding at the bottle.

And all was quiet, except for the little voice in my head. I had a bottle of water in my bag, but I was too busy worrying about the germ cloud.

Germs are in the world, and some of them are going to get me, no matter what. Maybe I should just relax. —Edward Grinnan

*Lord, You came into this world and walked among the sick,
never fearing. It's flu season again. Grant me protection,
but grant me also Your compassion.*

Make a change today, like altering your diet or starting or changing your exercise routine, to improve your health.

HOLD IT LOOSELY

"Do not worry about tomorrow, for tomorrow will worry about itself...."
—MATTHEW 6:34 (NIV)

A FOREST FIRE THAT HAD BEEN RAGING SEVERAL MILES AWAY FOR DAYS HAD jumped two parallel canyons and now threatened countless neighborhood homes. From our patio, I stood with the neck of my T-shirt pulled over my mouth in an attempt to filter the smoke in the air and stared at the tall, angry flames in the distance as they licked their way toward the sky.

My husband had declared it go-time, asking me to pack our bags and get ready to load up, but as I scurried through every room of our home, I reached for surprisingly few things: a stack of my old journals; my favorite sweater; my purse; Prisca's favorite stuffed dog, Ike; Perry's beloved baseball cap; a few changes of clothes; our toothbrushes; some pajamas; and books and snacks. What else did we need, really? What else made our life *life*?

I wandered back through the rooms before heading to the car, snapping photos of each space. There was artwork I treasured, clothing I adored, cookbooks whose recipes I'd made for years. That handmade afghan from Nana, the angel figurine from my mom, decades' worth of scrapbooked scenes. But these things proved ancillary to life that is truly life. If our house was to be consumed by fire, these things would go up in flames. And so I went ahead and said good-bye to all my stuff that's just stuff in the end. —ASHLEY WIERSMA

Father, help me to hold my stuff loosely today.

Know when it is time to give "your stuff" away. Begin today by offering something you no longer need to someone else.

WELCOMING GOD'S PROVISION

"Do not worry then, saying, 'What will we eat?'"—MATTHEW 6:31 (NAS)

ON THE PLANE HEADED TO IOWA FOR A CONFERENCE, I FELT A LITTLE anxious. Newly diagnosed with celiac disease, I had to think carefully about my food—nothing containing wheat or gluten for me. This new way of eating complicated life. *Will I have to endure questions and stares in restaurants?* I thought. *I have a few apples from home, but should I have brought more?*

That first day at the conference I met Cynthia. "Hi," she said. "I heard you have celiac disease. Me too. I brought some things to share."

"That is so kind," I said. I felt as I did on my first day of kindergarten when my new friend shared cookies from her lunch box.

Cynthia offered wheat-free granola, flourless brownies, and peanuts. "Take whatever you want. I have plenty."

Later in the cafeteria, I smiled at Cynthia as we filled our plates. As the conference organizers had promised, there was gluten-free food for us.

On the last night we joined a group at a restaurant. Someone had chosen a place with a gluten-free menu! I had a great time, but I had to leave a little early. Later that night I heard a knock on my hotel room door. It was Cynthia. "I brought you something. You missed dessert." Crème brûlée, three different flavors.

As I hugged Cynthia good-bye, my heart and tummy were both full. God had provided, and He had sent a new friend who understood. —JULIE GARMON

Lord, thank You for Cynthia, who's been there.

Do you have special dietary needs? Make a portable snack to take with you the next you attend an event where diet sensitivities are a concern.

ALWAYS WATCHFUL

He that keepeth thee will not slumber. —PSALM 121:3 (KJV)

I FLICKED ON MY FLASHLIGHT AND LOOKED AT THE CLOCK; IT WAS ONLY midnight. I plumped my pillow. My mind was spinning out of control with "what-ifs." Earlier that day my mare had given birth to Wind Dancer, a gangly-legged, floppy-eared red mule—my dream mule. The owners of the guest ranch where I worked had let me electric-fence a separate pasture away from their huge herd. It was the safest—and only—option available. But I knew the dangers of newborn colts and electric fences.

I rolled on my back. *What if Wind Dancer gets tangled up in the wire with the current shocking her? What if a deer runs through the fence and knocks it down and Wind Dancer escapes? Maybe I should check on them.* As I sat up in bed, my German shepherd groaned loudly, as if to say, "*Ahem,* I'm trying to sleep."

"Exactly, Tess, I'm trying to sleep too." Or was I? I had created a drama of "what-ifs," and nothing had happened—everything was fine.

There was one thing I hadn't done. *Lord, I'm worried about this electric fence. Please protect them.* Immediately, God's peace flooded my spirit and I fell asleep.

The next day I watched Wind Dancer zipping around the pasture. As soon as she approached the electric fence, her mom blocked her way. I watched as every time that red mule neared the fence, the mare herded her away.

I guess I'll never know if God gave the mare wisdom or if it was conditioning or instinct or His angels, but I did learn that when I gave my dramatized "what-ifs" to God, I could finally sleep. —REBECCA ONDOV

Thank You, Lord, for reminding me that there's
no sense in both of us being awake.

 Go over positive outcomes for all your what-ifs.

ROOM TO BE YOURSELF

If...you seek the Lord your God, you will find him if you seek him.
—Deuteronomy 4:29 (NIV)

My four-year-old son is busy. He climbs on furniture, has trouble sitting still for more than five seconds, and runs everywhere.

Most of the time I don't mind Trace's activity, but when he squirms during church, I lose my patience. Not only does he talk nonstop to anyone who dares to sit next to us, but he also dances during hymns and stands on the pew and says, "Amen!" as loudly as he can. I worry constantly that he is distracting the other worshipers. "Church is a time for quiet reflection," I whisper.

One Sunday our pastor asked Trace if he'd be willing to light the candles during the opening prayer. I was about to decline (picturing candle wax dripping down the aisle) when Trace said, "Please, Mommy, I know I can do it." He looked so excited that I didn't have the heart to say no.

The candles got lit. But it took two trips because Trace walked so fast the first time that the flame on the candle lighter went out. And he managed to get everyone laughing when he skipped back to his seat. *That's the last time I let him do that*, I thought.

Days later, Trace got a card from Nancy, a church member. "Dear Trace," it said, "thank you for the wonderful job you did helping your church family last Sunday. We all love the joy and enthusiasm you bring. You are a blessing."
—Amanda Borozinski

Dear Lord, help me to remember there is a place for all of us in Your family.

When you feel insignificant in the body of Christ, reflect on how God has made you feel like an important extension of His loving hand.

IT'S UP TO GOD

And he said, The things which are impossible with men are possible with God.
—LUKE 18:27 (KJV)

ONE OF THE SCARIEST TIMES FOR MY FAMILY WAS AWAITING THE BIRTH of my niece Kenedy. As it became clear that the pregnancy was incredibly dangerous for both mother and daughter, fear crept in. I would worry while I crocheted her blanket; I called every available minute for updates (even when I knew there were none); I stressed out every time I lost cell service underground on the subway.

I received some particularly bad news in a phone conversation with my brother. "The doctors said that there's very little chance the baby will survive, but it's not up to them. It's up to God."

This jolted me. I'd been stressing about something I couldn't control instead of talking with God about what He could do. I began to focus on prayers instead of worry, and claim the victory instead of assuming the worst. I silenced my doubting Thomas and worked on strengthening my faith. I prayed earnestly and directly to God. I was able to release the knot that had developed in my shoulders and then provide real support to my brother.

Before her birth, Kenedy was already giving me one of the greatest lessons I've ever been taught. —NATALIE PERKINS

Help me, Lord, to continue to see Your lessons in my life,
regardless of the source.

Has God taught you a lesson from an unlikely source? Let them know before night falls.

GOD CAN WORK IT OUT

Trust in the Lord with all your heart and lean not on your own understanding.
—PROVERBS 3:5 (NIV)

I CLICKED MY PEN AGAINST THE COUCH CUSHION AND STARED AT MY husband, waiting for him to respond. So far, the notebook on my lap was empty.

"I don't know," Ryan finally said.

I sighed. Earlier that day, we had officially decided to send out support letters for our adoption. We were sitting in our living room, attempting to make a list of people to whom we should send them. We weren't sure whether many of our aunts and uncles and cousins would understand our heart for the orphan.

We had already run into our fair share of interesting reactions when we announced our intention to adopt. Family members didn't understand why we would take this emotional and financial risk to travel to a war-torn country, just so we could bring some kid we didn't know into our home. Some of them looked at us like we were crazy.

Our worries reached their peak, so we put down the notebook and did what we should have done in the beginning. We prayed. And afterward, when we said our amens, Ryan looked at me. "God can work in any heart—even the ones we think are unlikely."

That afternoon, we sent out the letters to everyone. —KATIE GANSHERT

> *Forgive me, Lord, for all the times when I've let my fear and doubt limit Your power. Help me to be faithful with what I can control and trust You with the rest.*

✻ Promise yourself you'll spend fifteen minutes today focusing on what you can control. Entrust God with the rest.

TAKE IT SLOW

For many years you were patient with them.... —Nehemiah 9:30 (NIV)

I TRIED EVERYTHING: DEEP BREATHING, TEA, TAKING BREAKS TO GO ON walks. Nothing seemed to work.

I spent a couple of hours each day pounding my keyboard to write, and for some reason, it had been causing me a lot of stress and anxiety recently. My heart raced; my body tensed; my adrenaline flowed. However, my search for a remedy had, so far, come up short.

One night, at a neighborhood joint, I ordered the grilled asparagus, marinated in balsamic vinegar and sprinkled with Parmesan cheese, to go. When the chef handed me my meal, I thanked him.

"Take it slow," he said.

What a bizarre farewell, I thought to myself. *Take it slow.* The words felt unnatural to me, not only because I'd never heard anyone use them in that context before, but also because they were the exact opposite of the way I approach my work. I take it fast. I put my fingers on fully automatic and unleash a torrent of words as if my life depended on the volume of my output.

The next day when I sat down to write, I took it slow. I tried to work as carefully and deliberately as possible. And you know what? It worked. It wasn't easy. It felt inefficient and tedious, like signing my name with my left hand, but it worked. I'm calmer, more relaxed, more still before the Lord.
—Joshua Sundquist

Lord, please help me to take it slow.

Look at where being in a rush got some of the people in the Bible. Note the lessons when you start feeling impatient.

GOD HEARS THE GROANS OF YOUR HEART

We do not know what we ought to pray for, but the Spirit himself intercedes for us through wordless groans. —ROMANS 8:26 (NIV)

"C'MON, GUYS, IT'S TIME TO LEAVE!" I CALL. THE YOUNGER KIDS HEAD toward the door.

"No!" John bellows so loudly that Stephen clasps his ears. I take a deep breath. It's my fifteen-year-old's Sunday-morning anxiety attack, which manifests itself as belligerence. I have Andrew go on ahead with the other kids. It's better to handle this without an audience.

I talk to John for a bit. It is the usual problem: He is afraid God is angry and will not forgive him for some of the things he's done in the past. We talk about grace, mercy, and love. We discuss the irrationality of thinking you're the only unforgivable person in the world. I pray for him silently, because he won't let me pray out loud.

Then I have to decide: Is he safe and capable of calming down on his own? Should I stay home to make sure he's okay? I head out the door, hoping John will join us at church in a little while.

A deep ache grows in my heart as I walk the two blocks to church, the grief of a mother whose teenager's troubles stretch far beyond her ability to solve. I try to articulate my feelings in prayer but cannot. Not knowing what else to do, I shove the groan in my soul God-ward, as if to say, "Here. This is what I mean. You know." And God does. —JULIA ATTAWAY

Holy Spirit, speak the words I cannot utter.

Take a series of deep breaths. Imagine yourself releasing your concerns.

GOD OF JOYFUL SURPRISES

The world is established, firm and secure. —Psalm 93:1 (NIV)

It was one of those frustrating dreams where one vague scene dissolves into another and nothing makes sense. People I couldn't identify wanted me to do something—what it was, I couldn't discover. Indefiniteness—that was the nightmare part. *Where am I? Why do rooms keep changing? Why can't I stop one of these faceless people long enough to ask?*

Then the phone rang and I woke up. The floor was firm beneath my feet as I crossed my bedroom, the furniture reassuringly stationary.

"I'm sorry to call so early," my daughter began. She needed an address for a meeting that morning. She started to apologize again, but I was so glad for an actual conversation that I wouldn't have cared if it was 3:00 AM instead of 7:00 AM. After the call, I walked around the apartment, grateful for the real world of stable places and predictable sequences.

Dreams may express unrecognized anxieties: dread of old age as I enter my late eighties; fear of no longer being able to live up to the expectations of family and friends; a feeling that old people are ignored, that everything's moving too fast. What this dream gave me, though, was something more important: a joy I hadn't known existed. Joy in the real world: its solidness and reliability. Joy for God's orderly, beautiful, coherent creation. —Elizabeth Sherrill

God of joyful surprises, amid all the changes in my life,
let me cling to Your unchangingness.

Meditate on the meaning of "JOY"—Jesus, others, and you, in that crucial order.

WORRY IS A WASTE OF TIME

"Therefore do not worry about tomorrow, for tomorrow will worry about itself. Each day has enough trouble of its own."—MATTHEW 6:34 (NIV)

EACH SUMMER I HAVE THE OPPORTUNITY TO GIVE A KEYNOTE SPEECH AT A big conference. It's a lot of fun and significant to my career.

Pretty much from the second I walk offstage, I start brainstorming about what I will say in my speech the following year and continue to do so until the next summer rolls around. It's exciting to look forward to that speech! And I'm not worrying, after all. Worry is anticipating negative events; the conference is a positive.

A few days ago I was blindsided by the news that I was not invited to speak there this summer. After the initial wave of disappointment, the first thing I thought of was how much I had been consumed by the conference all year. Taken together, it must have been many hours, if not days—time I could have been thoughtfully engaged in that day's activities.

Worry is, at best, a waste of time and, at worst, a destructive, downward spiral of negative thinking, because the things we worry about often don't happen. This experience with the conference is teaching me that planning and fantasy—what we might call "positive worry"—isn't much better. The things I am looking forward to sometimes don't happen either, and if I fritter away hours in endless fantasy, I am misplacing my attention, missing out on what God has given me today, and not trusting Him to provide for me tomorrow.
—JOSHUA SUNDQUIST

Lord, please let me trust You with all of my hopes and fears.

Have you been "passed over" in an area of *your* life? Write down the name of the person who wounded you, finding something to praise in the situation. It will free you.

FOCUS ON TODAY

*Take therefore no thought for the morrow: for the morrow shall take thought for the things of itself.... —*MATTHEW 6:34 (KJV)

ON A DAY WHEN I WAS WORRYING TOO MUCH ABOUT MONEY—THE immensity of college tuition occupying too much of my brain—I stepped away from the computer and picked up an old family photo album.

There was a picture of William's pirate birthday party when he was five, his classmates dressed in eye patches and bandanas, brandishing plastic swords and searching for buried treasure. There was a shot of Timothy in white with a silver halo circling his blond head, the perfect angel dressed for the Christmas pageant. There were photos of the boys in their baseball uniforms and snapshots of us at picnics in friends' backyards—that was me pushing Tim in a swing, both of us laughing so hard you could see our tonsils. My eye lingered at the one of Carol and me sitting in beach chairs, the boys splashing in the bay, neither of us with a care in the world...

Until I remembered all the things I worried about that day at the beach, like how would we ever afford nursery school and would Timothy ever learn his colors and would William please get a base hit at least once. In fact, if I looked closely at the photos, I could recall worries that had plagued me at every moment—all the way back to the proud moment I first held William in my arms.

I closed the album and went back to the computer. *See,* I told myself, *you got through that just fine. You'll get through this too.* —RICK HAMLIN

Lord, I promise not to let worries for tomorrow
rob me of the pleasures of this day.

> Flip through a photo album and reflect on God's goodness in the times of your life.

FAITH IN GOD'S PLAN

Hezekiah trusted in the Lord, the God of Israel. There was no one like him among all the kings of Judah, either before him or after him. —2 Kings 18:5 (NIV)

Last year was a tough time, jobwise. I work for a large publishing company that was suffering from budget cuts and a lack of advertisers, the people responsible for putting pages in the books. Every month, it seemed, a large wave of pink slips arrived and e-mail notifications were sent of impending layoffs, shuttered magazines, and farewell lunches for coworkers.

At first I had dreams in which I saw myself working through the night. I'd wake in the morning and take medicine for the jaw pain I'd developed from grinding my teeth. And while work had once been a blissful place for seeing friends and exchanging ideas, it was now a tense place where everyone wondered what this Friday's company update would bring.

I sat at home one weekend, worried about what would become of my department, my coworkers, and my source of income, when it hit me: I was doing my very best. I was performing well at work, exceeding the goals set by my boss. What more could I do? At that moment, I gave my fears over to God and felt a wave of welcome peace wash over me.

When I returned to work on Monday after a delightfully dream-free weekend, I found that I could sit down and work through the day without worrying about who might be the next to go. I could only be responsible for myself, and with hard work and faith in God's plan, I knew I'd be fine. —Ashley Kappel

Remind me, Lord, to give my worries to You and
to trust You when I do.

Write the word *PEACE* in a journal or slip of paper. Find guiding principles to create an acronym for your life.

MORAL SUPPORT

Whenever I am afraid, I will trust in You. —PSALM 56:3 (NKJV)

RECOVERY INTERNATIONAL IS A FREE SELF-HELP GROUP FOR PEOPLE WITH anxiety or depression (or both) and was started decades ago in Chicago by the late Abraham Low, MD, a neuropsychiatrist who wanted to help his patients help themselves.

I sometimes pray for help with my anxiety and depression, so when a friend found a mention of Recovery International in *Dear Abby*, I went with her as moral support. I related, too, so I kept going back.

One of the group's tools for dealing with misplaced feelings is something called "spots," from the phrase "to throw a spotlight on." If I start to feel fearful about something, I can interrupt that thought with a spot. For example, "If you can't change a situation, you can change your attitude toward it."

I like to remind myself that I am not transparent. No one can see my inner feelings when I am shaky, like when I substitute-teach in a noisy high school classroom. Another helpful spot is "Feelings are distressing, but they are not dangerous." A favorite of mine: "Don't take your own dear self too seriously." The spots help stop the worry when it grows and starts to spiral downward.

One thing that hinders people from getting the help they need is being ashamed of their feelings, of not being perfect. I know what that's like, so I decided to pray that I would "not take my own dear self too seriously." —LINDA NEUKRUG

God, if there is something that has helped me and might help another today, please give me the strength to share it.

Did you know that worrying is fiction? The future doesn't yet exist, so worrying about it isn't based in fact. Change your worry today to simple concern, which is based in fact and focuses on the present.

PUT ANXIETY ASIDE

All the days ordained for me were written in your book before one of them came to be.
—PSALM 139:16 (NIV)

VISITING A MUSEUM, I PAUSED IN FRONT OF A PICTURE BY THE SURREALIST René Magritte. In the painting, an artist sits before an easel, staring at an egg placed on a table. On the canvas, though, he's not painting an egg but a feathered, full-grown bird.

Puzzling, when there were more than enough puzzles in my life just then! My husband and I were trying to sell our home of fifty years in the worst housing market in decades. Moving near family in another state meant leaving not only friends, but longtime doctors and dentists, service people, our church. How could we ever find replacements for these things? Which belongings could we take to a small apartment? How would we manage if the house didn't sell?

I turned away from Magritte's perplexing painting and then looked again. The artist in the picture, clearly, was painting not what he saw but what he knew. The beak, the claws, the feathered wings on his canvas—all this, in time, would develop from an egg. The artist saw the end from the beginning.

I'm seeing only the egg, I thought, things as they are at present. I can't see the life-in-the-making that will someday take shape. But there's an Artist at work in my life, and every life, One Who sees the completed picture and knows the people, the places, the specifics of a future still invisible to me. —ELIZABETH SHERRILL

*Help me put anxiety aside, Father, and watch Your brush
at work on the finished portrait.*

Study the tangled threads on the back of a piece of needlework. Then turn it over and admire the finished product. As you do, praise the Great Artist Who is at work in *your* life too.

RECEIVE THE BLESSING

Be still before the Lord and wait patiently for him.... —PSALM 37:7 (NIV)

TWO WEEKS AGO I WAS GOING TO A JOB INTERVIEW WHEN I REALIZED I'D forgotten to put on a belt. I rushed into a clothing store and picked up a new one, then found myself stuck in an incredibly long checkout line. I stood convinced I would be late. *This line is ridiculous! Why is everyone so slow?*

Finally I remembered to pray, and the anxieties racing through my mind were quieted. I found myself hearing the discussion at the front of the line.

"Are you sure? Can you check again?" a customer was asking.

"I've already checked twice for you and asked my manager. There is no match for that shoe," said the cashier. "Could you move, please? You're holding up the line."

The customer sighed, starting to walk away. "But what will you do with just a single shoe?" he asked.

"Throw it away probably," the cashier said.

"Excuse me," I said. "Is that shoe a left or a right?"

"A right," said the cashier.

"What size is it?"

"It's a ten."

"That's my size!" I said. "I'll buy it."

As an amputee, I usually have to buy a pair of shoes and throw one away, but that day I got a single shoe for just $2.12—all because I slowed down long enough to see a gift God had put in front of me. And as a bonus, I made it to the interview on time and got the job! —JOSHUA SUNDQUIST

Lord, help me slow down long enough to receive Your blessings.

 Take a deep breath and thank God for the blessing in front of you.

*Lord, I am overwhelmed. I have
too much to do, too many details
to remember and resolve, too many
demands on my time, and increasingly
limited energy and intelligence. Like the
psalmist and king, David, I feel besieged
and near defeat. Yet, also like David,
I realize that my worst enemy is often
myself. Help me to accept, dear Father,
that You are in charge. Give me rest
and clear up my confusion so that I put
You at the top of my list of priorities,
understanding that everything else will
then find its proper place. Amen.*

....

MARCI ALBORGHETTI

Chapter 5

WHEN YOU FEEL

DISCOURAGED

....

Disappointments are inevitable;
discouragement is a choice.

FROM *30 LIFE PRINCIPLES: A STUDY FOR GROWING*
IN KNOWLEDGE AND UNDERSTANDING OF GOD
BY CHARLES STANLEY

SIMPLE JOYS

"Thou didst clothe me with skin and flesh, and knit me together with bones and sinews." —JOB 10:11 (RSV)

SOME YEARS AGO I HAD WHAT THE QUEEN OF ENGLAND ONCE CALLED an *annus horribilis*, an awful year, when every bad thing that could happen happened: love died, relatives died, jobs died, cars died, things were as bleak as they could get. But oddly enough I learned a great happy lesson that year: I learned the simple joy of the body.

I remember one night in particular, when I was drowned in loss, I grabbed my basketball and dribbled down the street to the park and shot baskets all night long until the sun crawled up. I remember shooting and shooting until I thought my arm was going to fall off. This sounds like a totally ridiculous male way to deal with a crisis, but everyone has places they go when they are scared and exhausted, and that was mine then.

In the years since, through the deeper and harder losses of middle age, I have realized, year by year, almost day by day, the utter astounding gift of the sweet creaky vehicles issued to us by the Coherent Mercy. The intricacies of your fingers! The dart and dance of your tongue! The throb of your heart, the flash of your mind, the fact that your knees and elbows work! Isn't it astounding, when you think about it, that despite all the sickness and injury and wear and tear, we get these totally cool mammalian miracles to drive? —BRIAN DOYLE

Dear Lord, well, I have some questions about the design of the spine, and is this really the right size nose for this body? But other than that, boy, am I grateful for this body.

 Celebrate the gift of life by pushing yourself to accomplish something physical today.

LET GOD BE PRESENT

"And what does the Lord require of you but…to walk humbly with your God?"
—Micah 6:8 (NRSV)

Have you ever had one of those days when things don't go as planned? How did you handle it? I hope better than I did, as you will see.

I'd been asked by a church group torn by severe disagreements to mediate the situation, something I'd done a number of times before. I knew how this worked and what to do. Except this night, what I knew wasn't working. And the harder I tried—my original process, then Plan B and C and D—the more recalcitrant the participants got. Finally, I said, "We're going to take a break. Let's come back in fifteen minutes." But I didn't have a Plan E.

Outside, half-angry, half-crushed under the weight of my own failure, I said to God, *What do I do?*

The stars shone brightly, and for the longest time I just looked into the great expanse of heaven. As my shoulders sagged and my eyes teared, I found Plan E. I went back into that tense room and invited those people outside to look up. "I've been trying too hard to solve your problem and have simply gotten in the way," I said. "What if we start over? But this time let's remember how we fit in God's world."

We didn't fix everything that night, but in the next few weeks, tensions started to ease and enemies began to reach across the aisles. I got out of the way and let God be present. —Jeff Japinga

God, show me where I can step out of the way and
instead point to Your glory.

 Let go and let God. Right this very minute.

GRATEFUL-FOR-LIFE MOMENTS

I pray that the eyes of your heart may be enlightened in order that you may know the hope to which he has called you.... —EPHESIANS 1:18 (NIV)

A GOOD DOCTOR IS OFTEN MORE THAN A DOCTOR IN OUR LIVES.

At my husband Lynn's recent regular appointment with his neuro-oncologist, we talked about quality-of-life issues. Lynn has been on chemotherapy for more than a year for his brain tumor. When the doctor asked how things were going, I confessed that Lynn was saying the word *hopeless* more often.

The doctor swiveled his chair around and looked directly at Lynn. "I treat your cancer, but I also treat you as a person," he said, "and it's important to feel hopeful. In fact, if you reach the end of a day and can't think of the reasons you are glad you lived through that day, we need to make some changes."

He paused and then asked Lynn, "What feels hopeless?"

"That I may never feel better than I do right now," Lynn answered.

So the doctor outlined an option to cut back on some of Lynn's medications, including his chemotherapy doses. We readily agreed to make those changes.

Maybe even more important, we took the doctor's other suggestion, which had nothing to do with medications. At the end of the day, I try to remember to ask Lynn, "Why are you glad you lived through this day?"

The answers have varied: a grandchild's birthday celebration, voting, or clearing up an insurance snafu. But here's what has been most hopeful: For both of us, that question seems to open our eyes to all the possible answers tucked into each day. —CAROL KUYKENDALL

Father, may I embrace the grateful-for-life moments
You give me each day.

Initiate a gratitude journal. Each night before retiring, list five things God surprised you with that day.

FOCUS ON THE POSITIVE

The Lord has done it this very day; let us rejoice today and be glad.
—PSALM 118:24 (NIV)

LONGTIME MEMBERS OF MY SMALL CHURCH JOKE THAT ON SUNDAY mornings we celebrate holy Eucharist followed by holy coffee hour. After the dismissal, "Let us go forth into the world, rejoicing in the power of the Spirit," most of us file downstairs for snacks and conversation.

When welcoming newcomers, I focus on the positive within the church.

When I update friends who know the cyclical feast-or-famine nature of self-employment or ask, "What's new?" I veer toward the negative.

Then a month ago, I noted a quotation from Ingmar Bergman's classic *Fanny and Alexander*. At the climax of the film, a curmudgeon uncharacteristically pronounces, "Let us be happy when we are happy." Sounding so biblical, the "Let us" proclamation settled into my mind.

At the next coffee hour, with my friends Julia and Jane, I started with some version of "I'm all right but..." Then I corrected my course. "No," I said, "I'm not adding the *but*. I have plenty of work. I've had a good weekend. The sermon encouraged me." I quoted the line "Let us be happy when we are happy," and our conversation opened up. Jane reported that her unemployed daughter got an interview. Julia, who is downsizing, had worked through a closet. Slow and sure progress.

Since then, we intentionally encourage one another when leaving church to rejoice in the day, in the Lord, in the power of the Spirit. —EVELYN BENCE

Lord, help me claim the happy moments

 Just for today, when someone responds with a negative remark, counter with a sincere positive response.

A GIFT OF HOPE

Therefore encourage one another and build up each other, as indeed you are doing. —1 THESSALONIANS 5:11 (NRSV)

DO YOU TWITTER? ARE YOU LINKEDIN? DO YOU HAVE FRIENDS ON FACEBOOK?

I don't know about you, but I've been slow to adopt much of the social networking revolution on the Internet. I never could quite understand why a whole bunch of people would want—or especially need—to know what I'm doing or thinking in 140 characters or less. (That's Twitter, for those who don't "tweet.")

A great benefit of my work is that I get to hang around a younger generation. I sat with a group of them one night in the lounge of one of my school's residential buildings, so I started asking them about social media.

"Do you like people?" one of the students asked me.

"Well, of course I do," I said. "But what does liking people have to do with telling them everything all the time?"

She smiled. "Sharing hope and joy with people is a great gift. Why wouldn't I want to do that in every way I can?"

I'm still not convinced about social media. But I was convinced that night about something else: As a person of faith, I'm called to share my hope and joy with others, no matter how I do it. That's why every single day, whether on Facebook or face-to-face, I have a goal: offer five friends a kind word, a good thought, a gift of hope. —JEFF JAPINGA

Open my eyes today, O God, to those who need an encouraging word. And open my mouth (or move my fingers) so that I might offer it.

 Share face-to-face encouragement with a perfect stranger today.

SUSTAINED

Hear my prayer, Lord; listen to my cry for mercy. When I am distressed, I call to you, because you answer me. —Psalm 86:6–7 (NIV)

"Dad, how does prayer work?"

This morning I finished my breakfast and was on my way up the stairs for a shower when my daughter Christine came out of her bedroom and asked me this question. The look on her face told me it was serious and more than a theological question.

At first I wasn't sure how to respond. I stumbled along and then slowly began to say, "Sometimes we pray…and God gives us what we ask for. Other times the response takes longer or never seems to come. I'm not sure why…" While I was trying to say something that made sense, I could see that Christine was very upset.

She followed me into my room and said, "Dad, I keep praying for something, but nothing happens." Tears were streaming down her cheeks.

Once again I tried to find the right thing to say so that my daughter wouldn't lose her faith in prayer and, more importantly, in God. What I wanted to say but didn't was something I heard once from a Guideposts prayer volunteer: "I don't know *how* God is going to answer these prayers. But I do know that God answers them."

In spite of Christine's seemingly unanswered prayer, she hasn't stopped praying or believing—and neither have I. —Pablo Diaz

Lord, may Your love sustain me when my faith is weak.

✸ Keep a prayer journal of petitions answered…yes, no, and later. Take special notice of God's providential timing.

EMBRACING ENCOURAGEMENT

Two are better than one... —ECCLESIASTES 4:9 (ESV)

THE JOG I TAKE A COUPLE OF TIMES A WEEK FROM OUR HOUSE TO THE PARK, down through the Heather Garden and up around the museum—oh, that hill—doesn't seem to get any easier. When I think of the hundreds of times I've done this short run, I don't see why it should be such a challenge, but in the morning when I punch the alarm clock and pull on my sweatpants, it's as though I'm about to climb Mount Everest. The first few yards out of the driveway and up to the corner mailbox are excruciating.

Then something happens. I pass a neighbor walking her dogs and wish her good morning. I see a friend taking his two children to school and marvel at how tall they've grown. I notice the marigolds and dahlias that some intrepid urban gardener has planted beneath the sycamores. I wave to a hearty trio of walkers coming down the hill I'm about to climb. "Keep it up," we tell one another. Just when I don't think I'm going to make it, I hear footsteps behind me. "Hey, stranger," a voice says. It's Michael, one of the neighborhood dads I've hardly seen since our kids graduated from Little League. "Can I join you?"

We do the loop around the museum and take in an extra loop for good measure, something I would have never done without his encouragement.

"How was your run?" my wife, Carol, asks when I get home.

"Great," I say. "I caught up with the neighborhood." You can always travel faster and farther when you're with friends. —RICK HAMLIN

I thank You, God, for the friends who give me encouragement
and help me on my way.

 Have you lost contact with an old friend? Phone them today and leave an encouraging voice mail. They'll smile at the sound of your voice.

GLORIFYING GOD IN ALL THINGS

Lord, you establish peace for us; all that we have accomplished you have done for us.
—ISAIAH 26:12 (NIV)

RECENTLY MY WIFE, ROSIE, AND I ATTENDED A BOARD MEETING IN DENVER. As we sat around the table at lunch, people began to talk about their occupations and accomplishments. One woman, the wife of another board member, seemed reluctant to join the conversation. "I don't have any special gifts," she said.

Eventually in the course of our discussion, we learned that she had visited missionaries in Africa and was working on a study guide on the Gospel of Matthew for them. She had already written study guides for two other biblical books. We were amazed at her accomplishments.

"For a person without any special gifts," I said, "you surely are a blessing!" It was such an encouragement to meet someone who was being used by God in such a powerful way. But it also got me to thinking: Sometimes I may fail to celebrate the ways God is working in my life because I'm so focused on other people's accomplishments that I can't see my own. So now, whenever that happens, I pray. —DOLPHUS WEARY

Lord, in whatever I do, help me to glorify Your name.

 Take a good look inward. Marvel at what God has accomplished through the instrument of *you.*

FAITH PASSED ON

I am reminded of your sincere faith, which first lived in your grandmother
Lois and in your mother Eunice and, I am persuaded, now lives in you also.
—2 TIMOTHY 1:5 (NIV)

WHEN I WAS GROWING UP IN NEW YORK CITY, OUR SPANISH PENTECOSTAL congregation purchased the building adjacent to the church to expand its ministry. We were in the middle of the construction project to connect both buildings when they collapsed. Thankfully, no one was hurt.

As the news spread, newspapers, TV reporters, strangers, and our church family gathered in front of the rubble. It looked like a scene from a movie. Debris and mangled iron were everywhere, and dust rose up from where the buildings once stood. "What do you think is going to happen to our church?" my cousin Felix asked me.

His mother, Maria Antonia, cried, asking, "Will we be able to rebuild?"

Just when it seemed like a wave of sadness and fear was overtaking us, Pastor Pedro stood up. "I know that we are saddened by the collapse of our buildings and it may seem like our dream is shattered, but God is with our congregation. Our faith will see us through. Our prayers will keep us going."

That event took place more than forty years ago, but it is etched in my mind and heart. When I face challenges, and obstacles seem impossible to overcome, I remember the courage and resilience of those who stood on that city sidewalk—and I am encouraged to press on. —PABLO DIAZ

Lord, thank You for the faith passed on to me by my church family.

Remember a person in your church who accomplished great things for God. As you reflect on their courage and resilience, set a goal for yourself that seems unattainable. When you reach that goal, set another one, even higher.

GODLY FRIENDSHIP

"Abba, Father," he said, "everything is possible for you. Take this cup from me...."
—MARK 14:36 (NIV)

"FATHER...PLEASE TAKE THIS CUP OF SUFFERING AWAY FROM ME," JESUS pleaded in the darkening Garden of Gethsemane. No one can know what pain and grief lay behind those words, but they came suddenly and unexpectedly into my mind when my therapist told me quietly but firmly, "It's time for electroconvulsive therapy, Brigitte. You are losing this battle." Depression has shadowed my life for years, yet I'd always imagined I could endure it into defeat.

But now it was hard to eat, a major task to pick up a ringing telephone and, even worse, hard to feel the usual blessings of affectionate children and incorrigibly whining grandchildren. ECT is feared for its ability to wipe out short-term memory. But did I have a choice?

I trusted my therapist, so I took medical leave from work, even though I felt life as I had known it might be over.

I underestimated something simple and powerful: friendship. Led by a fellow depressive, my friends closed around me. Alice drew up lists of who would take me to the hospital, who would make sure I got home and how to reach my doctors. I knew memory might leave me, so I bought a large red notebook and resolved to write down everything before and during my treatment.

My notes tell me that my friends took time off work, rearranged their busy schedules, e-mailed one another with progress reports, and offered prayers. The curse of depression became the blessing of love. —BRIGITTE WEEKS

Thank You, Lord, for the faith and care of true friends.

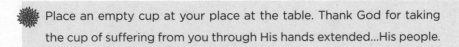 Place an empty cup at your place at the table. Thank God for taking the cup of suffering from you through His hands extended...His people.

PEACE, BE STILL

Then He arose and rebuked the wind, and said to the sea, "Peace, be still!"
—Mark 4:39 (NKJV)

When I was a boy, I preferred Sunday evening services because they were more informal. The song leader would often ask for favorites, and my hand would be the first one in the air. "Sing number one-oh-two, 'Master, the Tempest Is Raging'" (Mary A. Baker, 1874).

The dramatic song sent chills through me. It was about the disciples in the boat during a storm on Lake Galilee. When we got to the chorus, I would sing out like a drowning man:

Whether the wrath of the storm-tossed sea,

Or demons, or men, or whatever it be,

No water can swallow the ship where lies

The Master of ocean, and earth, and skies;

They all shall sweetly obey Thy will,

Peace, be still! Peace, be still!

I still think of that song when life gets stormy, when the winds of change rock my boat, when waves of anxiety wash over me, when I feel like I'm drowning in work, when the thunder and lightning of conflict frighten me. At such times I remind myself that nothing can sink my ship because Jesus is in the boat with me. He made the sea and the sky, and He can say, "Peace, be still!" and things will settle down. They always do. —Daniel Schantz

Father, the sea is big and my boat is small,
but I feel safe because You are here in the boat with me.

Find a picture of a raging sea today. Thank God that the One Who calms those storm-tossed waters lives in *your* heart.

ALL IS WELL

When my soul fainted within me I remembered the Lord.... —JONAH 2:7 (KJV)

I WOKE UP WITH A SHUDDER AS A FEELING OF IMPENDING DOOM SETTLED around me. The bad dream that had jolted me awake was receding, but it had clouded my usual optimism. Lying there in the dark, I was an easy target for the demons of worry and pessimism and hopelessness.

My mother is aging...what will life be like without her? How much longer can I manage to raise all the money we need for Zimbabwe? Our house needs so many repairs we can't afford. What if something bad happens to my children? What if I end up alone without David or too sick or too poor to care for myself? What if...? The longer I thought, the worse the what-ifs became.

There was only one thing left to do. I slipped out of bed and tiptoed out of the room, so I wouldn't wake my husband. I walked through the dark house and peered out the living room window. Ah, there it was. The moon. The night was chilly as I stepped out onto the deck, but the air made me feel real. I looked up at the sky and began to talk to God.

"Okay, I had a bad dream and I'm afraid. So many awful things can happen, things that I don't know how to handle. Are You here, God?" I waited. The moonlight shimmered through the trees. I kept waiting. A breeze, ever so slight, brushed against my face. I caught sight of one star and then another.

All is well, God seemed to say.

I enjoyed the night for a few minutes more and then went back inside. "All is well," I whispered. And I closed my eyes and went to sleep. —PAM KIDD

Father, even in the darkest night, let me remember You.

Before drifting off to sleep tonight, consciously shut out the negative thoughts that might disrupt your slumber.

FORGIVING MYSELF

"I do not say to you, up to seven times, but up to seventy times seven."
—MATTHEW 18:22 (NAS)

TODAY, IN GOING THROUGH MY "KEEP" PILE, I COUNTED FOURTEEN PAIRS of scissors: hot pink ones, neon green ones, tiny enamel babies I bought to clip thread, heavy-duty sewing models able to cut through any fabric. Some of the scissors are still in their original packages, a few I recognize as ones I purchased to give away (I guess I never did get around to it), and others I stocked in drawers throughout the cabin so I'd always have a pair handy.

Then there's the sunflower yellow jacket I bought at a clothing outlet for twelve dollars. The sleeves were too long, but it was a deep discount. When I got it home, I realized the alteration was too complicated for me and my sewing machine. I never did take the jacket to the tailor, and now it's out of style. I never wore the yellow and black beads I bought to go with it either.

I tossed the jacket and beads in the "Giveaway" pile and admonished myself. *Think of the food you could've bought for the hungry with all the money you wasted, Roberta.*

I wipe away tears of regret as I face the sin of my waste. *Dear Lord,* I pray, *help me to be more careful with money in the future. Please forgive me.*

And He does. Now I need to forgive myself. In the meantime, know anyone who could use a good pair of scissors? —ROBERTA MESSNER

Self-condemnation is spiritual clutter, Lord.
Help me to forgive myself seventy times seven.

Write the word *self-condemnation* on a slip of paper. Then snip it into small pieces with a pair of scissors, never to torment you again.

IT ISN'T ALWAYS WHAT
IT APPEARS TO BE

"What no eye has seen, what no ear has heard, and what no human
mind has conceived—the things God has prepared for those who love him."
—1 Corinthians 2:9 (NIV)

"It is what it is," a friend told me recently with tears in her eyes, as we stood outside aerobics class. She was describing her painful adjustment to a new reality in her life—impending divorce.

Though I knew those words helped her, I wanted to tell her how much I dislike that cliché, because it limits what "it" might become. I wanted her to believe that God could use this painful reality to grow something new and hopeful in her life, even though she couldn't possibly imagine how right now.

I know, because I've been there—not in the same circumstances, but with similar feelings. Three years ago, when I was diagnosed with stage IV ovarian cancer, I faced an emotional crossroad: I could resign myself to "It is what it is" or I could believe that "it" could become more than what appeared at that moment.

Once I got beyond the initial shock and grief, I recognized that cancer brought me opportunities and gifts most people don't have: the gift of experiencing deeper relationships with loved ones; the opportunity to choose to do what matters most each day; the strength to cope with hard realities.

As I left my friend in the parking lot, I prayed that she would receive the blessing of that same kind of hope—soon. —Carol Kuykendall

Lord, thank You for showing me that with You,
"it" isn't always what it appears to be.

 List three things inherent in a difficult situation in *your* life.

THE POWER OF LITTLE THINGS

"The little you had...has increased greatly, and the Lord has blessed you...."
—GENESIS 30:30 (NIV)

I JUST SPENT $43.87 AT THE DOLLAR STORE. HOW COULD I SPEND SO MUCH money at a place where things cost only a dollar? I went in to buy paper cups and craft sticks for a church project and Spanish moss if they had it. Maybe I'd stroll through the aisles and see if they had any pretty gift bags.

Turns out the store had all these things—and much more. Like this cool nail file that has green sparkly flowers on one side. Paper towels, sunglasses, a magazine that's only slightly out-of-date. Chewing gum. I even found a darling yellow straw hat for my granddaughter. And this purple plastic pill organizer that lets me put all my supplements for the week in one place.

Wait. I'm beginning to see how I could spend $43.87 at the dollar store. I did it one dollar at a time.

Little things tend to add up. A cookie here, some ice cream there—a pair of jeans that won't zip. A week too busy for devotional reading, a day so crowded that there's no time for exercise, an evening when one TV show turns into hours spent staring at the tube—then I wonder why I'm feeling sluggish, physically and spiritually.

But it works in a positive way too. One little act of kindness, one smile at a hassled clerk, one card sent to brighten someone's day—and the world doesn't seem as hostile, as hopeless. So here's to little things. Well managed, they can have big results. —MARY LOU CARNEY

Remind me, God, of the power of little things
done in Your name.

 Offer one act of kindness today that you don't tell a single soul about.

GOD IS ALWAYS LISTENING

I know that good itself does not dwell in me, that is, in my sinful nature. For I have the desire to do what is good, but I cannot carry it out. —ROMANS 7:18 (TNIV)

MY MOTHER-IN-LAW HAS ALZHEIMER'S DISEASE BUT STILL LIVES ON HER own in her house across the road from us. We are fortunate, compared to others with ailing parents. My husband can schedule his hours around his mom's needs and my job. Between the two of us, we are able to look after her.

I go by most afternoons to have coffee, fill her bird feeders, and bake corn bread or biscuits, her favorite foods.

Caring for my mother-in-law is idyllic enough. Little is expected of me beyond friendliness and patience. I routinely fail at both. Although it's not her fault she can't remember anything, I answer sourly when she repeats a question.

I am in constant prayer about my attitude. *Let me be loving in spite of myself,* I beg. *Give me patience.* God never seems to grant these requests.

Recently, she found a box under her sofa. We went through its contents.

In the box was a thank-you card I wrote years before. She had me read it out loud. In it, I apologized for my crankiness, "I want you to know I really love and appreciate you. I don't know what I'd do without you."

"Save that!" my mother-in-law said, snatching it from my hand.

Weird—and so cheering—how this note ministered to us both.

—PATTY KIRK

Holy and amazing God, Lord of what was, what is, and what will be, thank You for listening to me always. And for sending Your Spirit to interpret my groans. And for Your astonishing replies.

Go through a box of treasured mementoes today. Thank God for each one.

YOU ENCOURAGE US

Encourage one another and build each other up.... —1 Thessalonians 5:11 (NIV)

One May evening a few years ago, the phone rang. It was our daughter Danita, who is a pediatrician in Natchez, Mississippi. She said to her mother, "I just got the news about my cousin's heart attack and it bothers me. She's only a few years older than I am; she has a weight problem and so do I. I'm going to work to do something about my weight. Please pray, because I know it's going to be a long, hard process." Rosie assured Danita that we would pray with her and encourage her.

Danita joined a program and began to exercise, and by the next year, she had lost 112 pounds! We marveled at her determination, and she's been an awesome encouragement to friends, relatives, coworkers, patients, and also to us. Rosie was inspired to lose twenty-five pounds, and I've begun to walk more and eat more carefully.

The lesson we've learned from Danita is not just about losing weight; it's about discipline and faithfulness and being consistent in all that we do.
—Dolphus Weary

Lord, You are the faithful One. Thank You for using
our daughter to encourage us.

Make one tiny change toward an important goal. Keep at it, and three weeks later, add another one to your arsenal of change.

THE GIFT OF ENCOURAGEMENT

Your love has given me great joy and encouragement.... —PHILEMON 1:7 (NIV)

AT A RECENT SCHOOL BOARD MEETING, ONE OF OUR HIGH SCHOOL principals was promoted to supervisor. He stepped up to the podium to offer his thanks and acknowledged a former mentor who had encouraged him to get into administration. "You always have to have a person in your life who sees something in you that you don't," he said.

When I returned to college to complete a teaching certification, I was thirty years old, with four young children, sitting in classes with eighteen-year-olds who would say, "Yes, ma'am" or "No, ma'am" to me when I'd ask them a question. It was a trying first semester. College algebra was a challenge, since my last math class had been back in high school. I'd never been much of a science student, and my chemistry lab was difficult. When my English professor announced that no one had ever earned an A in her class, I was ready to drop the course. I ended up in my adviser's office, ready to quit college. I didn't think I could do it.

Thank goodness my adviser thought otherwise. His continued encouragement kept me in school, and in a few short years I'd graduated with honors, begun teaching, and even enrolled in graduate school. My adviser had seen something in me that I had not. —MELODY BONNETTE SWANG

Thank You, Lord, for the people in my life who encourage me to become more than I think I can be. May we all reach the glorious potential that You see in us.

Look for a hidden positive quality in a friend. Tell them about the strength you see in them that they may have missed.

HE GIVES INFINITE LOVE

One thing I know, that, whereas I was blind, now I see. —JOHN 9:25 (KJV)

ONE OF MY FAVORITE AUTHORS IS THE LATE ROBERT PENN WARREN. A writer of fiction, poetry, and literary criticism, he was awarded three Pulitzer prizes and was selected to be Poet Laureate of the United States.

Recently I learned that when Robert was in high school, he dreamed of attending the United States Naval Academy and becoming a career naval officer. Accepted by the academy, he was elated and spent his senior year of high school preparing mentally and physically for the challenge. Several months before graduation, Robert was playing with his younger brother, who threw a lump of coal at him. The jagged coal hit Robert in the eye, permanently limiting his vision and shattering his dreams of attending the academy.

Attending Vanderbilt University the next year, Robert floundered for direction and a new ambition. Always an avid reader, he was naturally attracted to literature and soon began to write. Gradually his talent emerged, and Robert's life turned in a direction he had never considered. The blinding of an eye had created a new vision.

We can be sure that a God of infinite love never causes our tragedies and losses. But God is always the God of another chance. God is faithful to create order out of chaos, goodness out of tragedy, resurrection from our most agonizing crucifixions. —SCOTT WALKER

Father, when the brightness of my vision dims,
help me to trust that You will restore my sight and
cause me to dream again. Amen.

 Think of a moment when a dream of yours got derailed. Let amazement fill your spirit with the way God birthed a new dream inside of you.

IN HIS OWN TIME

And the leaves of the tree are for the healing of the nations.
—REVELATION 22:2 (NRSV)

I'M ONE OF THOSE PEOPLE WHO CAN GET REALLY DISCOURAGED WHEN I can't see how the things I do are making a difference. But there's an antidote to my occasional descent into self-pity. His name is Nelson Henderson.

A friend lent me his dog-eared, slim volume of Henderson's *Under Whose Shade: A Story of a Pioneer in the Swan River Valley of Manitoba.* "It might help," was all he said, something I was seriously doubting halfway through the simple story. Until I hit the punch line of the book: "The true meaning of life is to plant trees under whose shade you do not expect to sit."

Henderson's medicine is simple. On those days when I know I'm especially susceptible to discouragement, I'll take a fifteen-minute break in the shade of a beautiful, nearly hundred-year-old maple tree just outside my home, where I can pray and be reminded: God will indeed use what I do in His name...in His own time...the right time. I let the majesty of the tree remind me of the majesty of God. —JEFF JAPINGA

> *God, help me to see my work not only for its immediate*
> *outcomes but for its impact generations from now,*
> *when someone else will enjoy its shade.*

Is there a book that has coached you throughout your life? Write the author and tell them so.

FAITH HEALS ALL WOUNDS

Lord my God, I called to you for help, and you healed me. —PSALM 30:2 (NIV)

DRESSED FOR YARD WORK, I WENT OUTSIDE AND FETCHED THE wheelbarrow. Yesterday was the anniversary of my sister's death, and I needed to be outside to think things through.

As I walked through our yard, I picked up sticks that had fallen during the harsh months of the winter. A favorite of mine, a gnarled old apple tree in the far corner of our field, lost a heavy limb. The maples and ash trees lost small twigs. I picked up the sticks and looked closely at the small buds of new growth.

Last winter was tough. Harsh winds and an early, heavy, wet snow did a lot of damage. I thought about yesterday. My family had gathered at the cemetery. We flew kites in memory of my sister. My son played a hymn on his trumpet while we sang. As the music filled the air, I felt better. It seemed the weight of our loss had lightened, shifted to grace and gratitude of the memories we have of her.

I walked the perimeter of our yard, picking up sticks. The first year of Maria's death, I wondered if I'd ever feel normal again. For months, I was plagued with a terrible feeling that another tragedy was looming.

Some say time heals all wounds, but I think it's faith. I looked down at my full wheelbarrow of dead wood. The storms of life spiritually prune me, tearing away doubt and fear. —SABRA CIANCANELLI

*Dear Lord, help me to break free of the deadwood
that blocks me from Your presence.*

Add broken twigs to a floral arrangement in your home. It will give height to the bouquet and assure you of God's pruning power.

GIVE LOVE

Meditate on these things; give yourself entirely to them... —1 TIMOTHY 4:15 (NKJV)

HENRY, MY CLOSEST FRIEND, SERVED AS SUNDAY SCHOOL SUPERINTENDENT at our church. When Henry asked me to teach a class, my firm refusal was laced with guilt. *Me teach? The children deserve better than that.*

Then one Sunday, when I was hurrying down a hall in the church basement, I passed a darkened classroom and heard a muffled cry. I entered the barren room where a single light bulb dangled from the ceiling. Two long tables filled the room, and a solitary window peeked down at the tables and out across the lawn. A little girl was huddled, weeping. I placed my hand on her shoulder. She glanced up, and between sobs she told me that her mother had died two weeks before. I hurried up the stairs to tell Henry I would try to teach.

Several Sundays later there was a knock on the classroom door before class began. I answered, and our assistant minister called me into the hall. "Oscar," he said, "always remember that the love you show these children on Sunday morning might be all the love they receive the entire week."

My mission was clear: I could share and I could listen with all my heart. The children showered me with attention, trust, and love. Some remained after class to share their concerns. We needed each other. —OSCAR GREENE

Caring God, thank You for using my efforts to strengthen and encourage young hearts to strengthen and encourage me.

 Do something today you don't really want to do. Look for God's Eternal Plan in your effort of love.

NUDGES FROM GOD

A word of encouragement does wonders! —PROVERBS 12:25 (TLB)

WHEN KINCAID, A YOUNG MAN IN OUR CHURCH, ENTERED AIR FORCE basic training, his parents distributed information so the congregation could write to him. I put the paper on my desk but didn't write. What could I say that would interest a guy right out of high school? It would be easier to just pray for him, so I added him to my list.

A few days later, a Guideposts reader phoned. "I told my husband I appreciated the way you shared your faith struggles," she said, "and he suggested I look up your number and let you know. I hope you don't mind." Of course I didn't mind! I was delighted she took the time to call. Then I got a text from my grandson David: "How r u? Ok I hope. Luv U!" It was short and sweet but warmed my heart.

Were these nudges from God? If I was cheered by knowing others were thinking of me, wouldn't Kincaid be as well? So I wrote to him, giving scores from the high school basketball games, a weather update, and telling him I prayed for him daily.

Prayer is still the most important thing I can do for others. But when Kincaid's dad reported that the letters he received provided encouragement during an exhausting and difficult boot camp, I realized that there were also times when my prayers needed to be signed, stamped, and delivered. —PENNEY SCHWAB

Thank You, Jesus for reminding me that prayer accompanied
by action is often the most powerful prayer of all.

Pray for a perfect stranger today.

COURAGE TO REACH OUT

Therefore, as we have opportunity, let us do good to all people, especially to those who belong to the family of believers. —GALATIANS 6:10 (NIV)

WHEN I RESIGNED AS PASTOR OF A CONGREGATION, ONE OF THE MOST disappointed folks was Bob, a good friend of several years. He couldn't understand why I was stepping down. On several occasions I felt his frustration, hurt, and annoyance and was saddened by his behavior toward me. We were not able to talk about our feelings before I left.

One afternoon while I was at my new job, I learned that Bob was in the hospital. I tried unsuccessfully to contact members of the congregation to learn more about his status. I even called him, but he didn't pick up. Finally, I sent him a text message: "Bob, thinking of and praying for you."

Early the next morning, I saw that Bob had responded to my message: "I am leaving the hospital today. Thank you for your prayers." I wanted to see him but felt like I had missed the visiting window since he was being discharged. My wife encouraged me to go.

When I arrived, Bob was surprised and happy to see me. Tears rolled down the corners of our eyes as we hugged. We talked, laughed, and caught up on family, church, and work.

I stayed with him and his wife until he was released from the hospital. On my way home, I thanked God we were able to put our disappointments behind us and reconcile our differences. —PABLO DIAZ

Lord, give me the courage to reach out to those
who have been disappointed or hurt by me.

Make a gentle move toward reconciliation with someone who has offended you.

SPREAD ENCOURAGEMENT

Those who are wise understand these things; those who are discerning know them.... —HOSEA 14:9 (NRSV)

MY FRIEND KELLY AND I HAVE PESSIMISM IN OUR DNA. IT IS SUCH A RELIEF to have someone to talk to who understands! Our conversations are a dark comedy that only we can see the humor in. "Who are you going to vote for?" one of us will ask. "*Phhsh,*" the other will answer, "why not just flip a coin?" On the sunniest day of the year, we're scanning the forecast for the next storm. Our discussions often begin with "Don't you just hate it when...?"

But there is one difference that we've come to accept: I have a deep faith and attend church regularly; Kelly doesn't.

One night we were talking in the usual vein when Kelly hesitated. "Um, I'm on a new kick," she said. "I'm trying not to be negative."

What? I almost demanded, but her tone shifted, so I waited.

"I don't want to get older and be angry and bitter," she explained. "But it's not easy to change."

She was right. Earlier in the year, I had tried to avoid saying one negative thing every day. It hadn't been easy, and I'd since let the practice slip. "Maybe I'll try again," I told Kelly.

She was pleased. "It should be easier for you, with your faith."

Though she'd meant it to be encouraging, it hit me full-force. True faith does not indulge negativity, and neither should I. —MARCI ALBORGHETTI

Lord, help me to remember: If you can't say something good,
don't say anything at all.

 Refuse to be negative and don't tell anyone about your new philosophy.

GOD IS THE LIGHT

"See, darkness covers the earth and thick darkness is over the peoples, but the Lord rises upon you...." —ISAIAH 60:2 (NIV)

THE GOLDEN GLOW OF DAWN CROWNED THE MOUNTAIN. I DRUMMED MY fingers on the steering wheel of the pickup. A cloud of dust swirled behind the horse trailer as I barreled down the dirt road to the trailhead. It'd been a long week at work. My income from my commission-sales job had plummeted because of the downturn in the economy. All my joy was gone, and I viewed myself as a failure. I couldn't wait to unload my horse for an all-day trail ride.

The road meandered through a gully. The truck chugged through the curve and up a steep hill. Suddenly, the sun popped over the mountain. It reflected off the dust on the windshield and blinded me with seven thousand pounds of horse trailer pushing me. Frantically, I grasped the steering wheel and floored the brakes. The truck and trailer skidded to a stop.

I leaned my head against the window. My heart pounded. For a second I was blinded to the world. All I could see and think about was the light.

I sighed. *That's what I need to do. God is the Light. Focus on His Word.*

I had lost my peace because I was focused on failure. But I hadn't failed because I hadn't quit. After my horseback ride, I found encouraging Bible verses and meditated on them daily. At work, I expanded in new directions. It wasn't long before I was wrapped in God's peace once again. —REBECCA ONDOV

Lord, thank You for showing me how to persevere
by reflecting on You.

 Put your arms around yourself and imagine they are God's arms hugging you. Relax in that peace.

Loving Creator, in Your goodness You have allowed others to recognize my worth and successes.

I sincerely thank You for that. May I never forget that all my abilities come from You.

Be with me in the days ahead so that my decision making will be rooted in Your wisdom. May all that I do be praise for Your glory.

....

VICKI ZURLAGE

Chapter 6

WHEN YOU ARE GRIEVING

....

Loss is nothing else but change,
and change is Nature's delight.

Marcus Aurelius

GOD'S COMFORT

"Let not your hearts be troubled; believe in God, believe also in me. In my Father's house are many rooms; if it were not so, would I have told you that I go to prepare a place for you?" —JOHN 14:1–2 (RSV)

WE STOOD AT THE CEMETERY BY MY FATHER'S OPEN GRAVE. THE DAY BEFORE, we'd had the memorial service at church with hymns and eulogies and hundreds of people bidding Dad a fond farewell. Now it was just family and that aching sense of loss.

Our friend Rick Thyne led the graveside service. "At church when I was a kid," he began, "we had a balcony that wrapped around the sanctuary. If I had to lead a prayer or read a psalm, I could look up and see the people who cared about me. They were my encouragers, urging me on. They believed in me and looked out for me. I thought of them as my balcony people."

I thought of Dad, asking me about my job or school or the kids and then hanging up the phone with his standard line, "Love ya."

"Your dad is not here," Rick went on, "but he can become one of your balcony people. He's there watching it all, taking it in." I could see Dad's smile, hear his laugh, remember his kiss on my forehead when he'd put me to bed. "You can let go of him in life as you hold on to all the good things he wished for you and made happen when he was here."

The front row of my balcony. Still there. Love ya. —RICK HAMLIN

Thank You, Lord, for all the people who formed me.
May I honor in life all they gave me.

 Do something to make a person close to you smile in memory of one of your "Balcony People."

COMFORT IN TRANSITION

Jesus said unto her, I am the resurrection, and the life: he that believeth in me, though he were dead, yet shall he live. —JOHN 11:25 (KJV)

A FEW YEARS AGO GUIDEPOSTS PUBLISHED *COMFORT FROM BEYOND*, A BOOK filled with warm and wonderful stories of the encouragement and solace people have received from family and friends who have passed on. I loved the stories, but I was skeptical that such a thing could ever happen to me.

Then one day a large brown envelope arrived in the mail. I opened it. There in my hand was a red file folder; "Brigitte" was written on the tab. A small sticky note attached to it said, "We thought you might like to have this."

Inside was a collection of poems, e-mails, photographs, a couple of newspaper clippings—everything that I had ever sent to my late friend and colleague Van Varner. Tears rolled steadily down my cheeks. *Van cared enough about* me *to save all these things?* There were painful reminders of how much I missed our bimonthly lunches, the restaurant in an old-line department store, where he always ordered the chicken-and-rice soup. And there was the knowledge of how steadily he had supported me both professionally and personally.

From that moment on there's been not a trace of doubt in my mind that Van is waiting for me, with his silver hair a little ruffled as he walks always on the curbside of the street "to have my sword hand free," as he used to say, though highwaymen are scarce on New York City's Fifth Avenue. —BRIGITTE WEEKS

Comfort and sorrow make for odd bedfellows, Lord,
but no one ever claimed that life was simple. And thank you, Van,
for that comfort from beyond.

 If you're missing someone who has passed from this earthly life, ask God for a sweet reminder of them.

HEALING EMOTIONAL HURTS

He heals the brokenhearted and binds up their wounds. —PSALM 147:3 (NIV)

IT HAD BEEN MORE THAN A YEAR SINCE OUR SON PAUL WAS IN A CAR accident, an accident so brutal it severely injured all involved—and killed a passenger in the other car. Paul's physical recovery was amazing, given the extent of his neck injuries. Within three months, he was back at the office, driving two hours round-trip to work, and working out in the gym. However, Elba and I wondered how he was doing emotionally. We were constantly praying, "Lord, help our son express his emotions from the accident. Heal him on the inside as well."

One evening, I inquired how the civil case was going. "Paul, did you call the lawyer?" "No," he replied. I pressed on: "You know, it is important that you call him and stay up-to-date on this matter." I sensed his lack of interest in the topic. I persisted: "Paul, you need to be responsible and reach out to him." The look in his eyes told me that I had crossed the line.

Standing tall with tears in his eyes and anger in his voice, he said, "I just want this thing to be over with."

His mom quickly responded, "Paul, we know that you are struggling and want to put all of this behind you. How can we help you?" There was a long pause. He finally answered, sharing his feelings for the first time since the accident, grieving for everyone affected—particularly the deceased.

Our prayers were answered. We now knew how much Paul had been hurting. This was the beginning of his emotional healing. —PABLO DIAZ

Lord, heal my hurts, especially those deep within me,
unknown to those around me.

 Spend time today seeking closure regarding something that is troubling your spirit.

IN DARK TIMES

*I, even I, am he that comforteth you.... —*ISAIAH 51:12 (KJV)

I POINTED MY RENTAL CAR EASTWARD THROUGH THE EARLY MORNING clouds draping the San Francisco Bay Bridge. I was rushing out to a hospital in San Pablo to see my friend Van, who had collapsed from a stroke a few days before while waiting to board a cruise ship bound for New Zealand. I was told he was in bad shape. I thought I might wait until they brought Van back to New York City, but a voice said, *No, you must go to him.*

What if he doesn't know me? What if he is completely unresponsive? The mere thought of Van, one of my oldest and dearest friends, not even recognizing me was devastating; the thought that he might die, unthinkable.

I parked my car in the crowded hospital lot. Every step toward the entrance was an effort. I was afraid to face the worst. *God, please help me do this.*

Van was alone when I got to his room. I spoke to him. No response. I leaned over and looked at his eyes. Closed. His mouth was open and his breathing ragged. My worst fears were coming true, and somewhere deep inside me a sob began to form. I slipped my hand around his. "Van..."

And I felt it, all the way up through my arm: Van's strong, hard grip. I felt it all the way to my heart. Then he pulled my hand to his lips and held it there.

He didn't open his eyes or even speak. But he didn't need to.

—EDWARD GRINNAN

Dear God, You guide us through the fog of our deepest emotions
and give us clarity when all seems dark and hopeless.
With You there is always comfort.

Remember a moment when you communicated with someone without words. Use another way to say "I love you" without saying it today.

LOVE DURING TOUGH TIMES

[Love] always protects, always trusts, always hopes, always perseveres.
—1 CORINTHIANS 13:7 (NIV)

MELISSA HAD WORKED IN GUIDEPOSTS OUTREACH MINISTRIES WHEN SHE became ill with cancer. Shortly after this diagnosis, my colleague Rhonda and I went to the hospital to meet with Evelyn, Melissa's mother, during Melissa's last days. Although Evelyn was in emotional turmoil watching her only daughter die, she welcomed us with great love.

During the funeral service, I shared a story about how Melissa loved her ten-year-old son. I turned to him and said, "Jake, your mom loves you. She always bragged about your football practices." Melissa dreaded going to practices, but she endured them to watch her little boy play. She knew the importance of being there for her son.

Two years later, at an Outreach event, Rhonda said, "Melissa's mom was looking for you but had to go. She asked me to give you this card."

"Dear Pablo," Evelyn wrote, "I will always appreciate the memories of love and compassion you gave to my daughter, Missy. I will also cherish the stories you told and the kind words you gave to Jake."

The irony here was, I was the one who was appreciative. I remembered the love Evelyn had shown to Rhonda and me. How, despite her great loss, Evelyn had the ability to love others. Melissa and Evelyn inspired me, for the love they displayed through action, for the love that lives on. —PABLO DIAZ

Lord, teach me to love those around me, even when life is tough.

When someone you love passes away, send a note recalling a specific memory to their family.

PAIN RELIEF

A time to rend, and a time to sew... —ECCLESIASTES 3:7 (KJV)

WE JUST RETURNED FROM MY HOMETOWN IN NEBRASKA WHERE WE attended the funeral of my brother's wife. They'd been married only eighteen months before her death from acute leukemia.

Don rarely shows his emotions, so I was surprised to see him drying his eyes on his handkerchief all through the service. Later, his eyes grew teary whenever he tried to talk about Doris.

Sometimes I think it would help, when we're hurting deeply, if we could do something explosive to get the pain out. I'm not advocating tearing one's clothes, as was the custom in Solomon's day, but just some harmless physical action that could help relieve that bottled-up pain.

What I like about this passage in Ecclesiastes is that after the intensity of clothes-tearing, there is "a time to sew" (though I'd prefer the word *mend* because it suggests healing). Before Doris died, she said to Don, "Be happy please. Do it for me." So my prayer question today is, "How do you sew up a broken heart? How can I help my brother heal?"

The answer is short—HELP—but the medicine is effective:

*H*old the torn cloth, the hurting one.

*E*ncourage him to talk about his pain.

*L*isten with all your heart, soul, and spirit.

*P*ray for his wholeness. —MARILYN MORGAN KING

Loving Father, may I remember to Hold, Encourage, Listen, Pray.

 For someone in your life who is coming apart at the seams, give them a pocket sewing kit. Tuck in a note that you will be holding them up in prayer as the Lord heals their heart.

GRACE AFTER LOSING LOVE

Give thanks unto the Lord, call upon his name, make known his deeds among the people. —1 Chronicles 16:8 (KJV)

"Brock, you have to tell this story," my client Judy said. "You have to tell it to everyone."

I'd been telling her what had been happening over the past six months: a broken engagement; a seemingly futile trip to Freeport in the Bahamas; an overwhelming feeling that redemption would be found in the fulfillment of a dream from a childhood filled with reading Ernest Hemingway and Jack London; a once-in-a-lifetime adventure in Mozambique, from which I'd returned a new man who was making a new beginning.

Judy had seen miracles before. She had moved to my hometown of Nashville, Tennessee, after her husband lost a two-year battle with cancer.

"You know, Brock, I used to pray that God would take care of him," Judy said. "It wasn't until after he was gone that a friend helped me realize that God had actually answered my prayers. He had taken care of my husband, just not in the way I'd wanted Him to. Sounds like God has taken care of you, too, Brock. You owe it to Him to let people know what has happened to you."

Judy was right. I had already shared my story with a few other people, and they had similar responses. But I was beginning to see that this wasn't just a personal, sometimes painful, story about a relationship gone bad; it was about finding a fuller, more abundant life. —Brock Kidd

Lord, how can I have gone in such a short time from the depths
of heartbreak to a new life of service? Only by Your grace.

> Think back on a sermon you've heard on the abundant life. Then open your spirit to the full future God has in store for you.

FOCUSING ON LIFE

For whether we live, we live unto the Lord; and whether we die, we die unto the Lord: whether we live therefore, or die, we are the Lord's. —ROMANS 14:8 (KJV)

RECENTLY I'VE DEALT WITH THE LOSS OF SEVERAL LOVED ONES. I INCLUDE in that tearful list my beloved cocker spaniel, Sally Browne, who went to her reward at age sixteen. She died in my arms on a beautiful May morning when once she would have streaked through the woods out back, flaxen ears flying and tongue lolling out, chasing some enthralling scent no mere human could hope to apprehend. Those years had long since passed for Sally, and finally, that May morning, I brought her to her vet's office. As her life slipped away, I felt the warmth and weight of her body fully against me. The vet put a stethoscope to her chest and whispered, "She's gone."

Gone is a hard concept. Every part of us rebels against it. When I think of my friend Van, whom I also lost, I'm tempted to think of a great emptiness where his presence once was. I knew him better than I knew most people, and he me. To lose him was incomprehensible, as if I'd lost a part of myself.

Yet loss *is* comprehensible, but only through the presence of God in my life, Who gives both life and death. To accept death, to accept loss, is to move past my pain and embrace God, trusting in His perfect love and comfort. Only He can bridge that cold gulf between loss and life, and help me forge pain into acceptance. It's only then that I can focus not on the one who died, but on the one who lived. —EDWARD GRINNAN

Lord, help me find the Presence that will never fade or die,
Who is there for Van and Sally and all who have gone ahead.

Ask God to give a message of love to a precious one who has gone on to heaven.

HEALING THE WOUNDED

If your enemies are hungry, give them bread to eat; and if they are thirsty, give them water to drink. —PROVERBS 25:21 (NRSV)

WE PROBABLY ALL KNOW SOMEONE WHO HAS BEEN AFFECTED BY VIOLENCE or war. You may have lost a son or daughter, a niece or nephew or grandchild in Iraq or Afghanistan. Or you may have been there in support of a friend who lost someone. If my friend Bill hadn't experienced this sort of loss himself, I don't think that a Bible verse could have possibly made him as angry as this one from Proverbs did.

Bill lost his son in the fighting in Afghanistan almost four years ago. Not a week goes by that he doesn't break down in tears—the sort of thing that Bill had never done before tragedy entered his life.

Bill and I were in Bible study together, and our leader was reviewing all of the passages in Scripture that talk about loving and praying for our enemies. In addition to the verse above, we also heard, "But I say to you, Love your enemies and pray for those who persecute you" (Matthew 5:44, NRSV). Even though those words come from the Sermon on the Mount preached by Jesus Himself, they infuriated Bill for a long time.

I'll tell you what: God works miracles. After weeks of seeking God's help, Bill is praying once again, and he tells me that praying for the men who killed his son has begun to heal his own wounds. —JON SWEENEY

Dear Jesus, when sorrow makes me feel like lashing out,
grant me the gift of forgiveness.

Next time you see a man or woman in uniform, thank them for their sacrifice to America. Better yet, ask them about their service.

HE IS THERE

The Lord is close to the brokenhearted and saves those who are crushed in spirit.
—PSALM 34:18 (NIV)

IT HAD BEEN A YEAR SINCE MY WIFE JULEE'S BROTHER MICK TOOK HIS LIFE after a long and only occasionally hopeful struggle with alcohol, drugs, and depression. It ended one June day with a bottle of pills. No notes. No more pain. Julee would sometimes talk about finding the manuscript to some masterpiece Mick left behind and getting it published. Then she would catch herself; that book had been buried with him. Her voice would trail off.

On this first June day without Mick, I found Julee sobbing on the bed. Not healing tears. Tears of anguish and bitterness. "I'm so angry," she said. "I don't even know who I'm angry at. Mick? God? Who says there are stages of grief…like there's some sort of GPS for your pain? There isn't. Don't believe it. There's just hurt, confusion, and loss that I will never ever understand!"

I didn't have an answer for Julee. I don't think she expected one. She needed to say what was in her heart, and her heart would change with time. She would always love her brother, and sometimes God is the only one big enough to be mad at in the face of such pain. A wise man in an AA meeting told me that life doesn't get easier, but it does get better. It took me years to understand that. Julee understood it too, even if she didn't feel it on this first June day without her beloved brother. But she would, in God's time. —EDWARD GRINNAN

Lord, life is not always easy, but when we walk with You
it is always good. Please be with Julee and those whose hearts grieve.

Grief is the price we pay for love. Reread the account of Jesus's death and imagine what it was like for those who loved Him on earth.

FROM MOURNING TO DANCING

A time to mourn, and a time to dance. —ECCLESIASTES 3:4 (NKJV)

I WAS NAPPING WHEN THE PHONE RANG. "I'VE GOT BAD NEWS," SAID MY brother. "When I stopped to see Mother, I found her on the floor. She'd apparently fallen and hit her head on a table corner. She's dead."

Mother was seventy-six, in reasonably good health and still living comfortably alone. My brother, a doctor, stopped to check on her every day at noon. On this day she was suddenly gone. No last hug, no regretful good-bye.

I missed her most painfully whenever something good happened. My first thought was, *Oh, Mother will be so pleased!* But I couldn't tell her. She was gone.

I have learned something about mourning. My question is "How does a grieving person move from mourning to dancing?" The Voice within replies:

I feel your pain and grief, My child,
for death has walked before Me too.
It takes away your loved ones
to where you cannot follow.
But you can choose to dwell
in loving moments lived,
or cling to sorrow and live a broken life.
You can choose to cling to your loss
or you can learn to dance again. —MARILYN MORGAN KING

> *O Holy One, comfort all who grieve today. Hold them close till they*
> *can once again make the choice for life. Then let the dance begin!*

 Write a letter to someone who has passed on. Let that be part of your healing process.

A NEW AVENUE

The Lord gave Job twice as much as he had before. —JOB 42:10 (KJV)

HERE NEAR OUR FRIENDS' HOUSE THE SHORE IS ALL ROCKS, WITH NO PLACE to walk. But a short path along the bluff leads to a long, sandy beach. Or it did, in other years.

Even before unpacking the car, John and I set out down that path, eager to stretch our legs after the five-hour drive. We were stopped short by an impassable jumble of rocks left by a winter storm.

The blocked beach access, I thought, was just one more example of how cherished things can be snatched away. The recent death of a close friend had made me extra-sensitive to any loss—like our dogwood tree back home, killed by invading beetles. Even the closing of a favorite bakery seemed part of the pattern.

A few days later we found a roundabout way down to the beach. Finally we could make our customary walk to the outlet, our reluctant turnaround point, a broad stream where a swamp emptied into the ocean. But...

"Surely," said John when we'd walked for twenty-five minutes, "we should have come to the outlet by now!" But the beach stretched on unbroken; before us lay miles of sandy coastline we'd never before explored. The same storm that had blocked the bluff path had sealed off the outlet and opened a new walking route.

When God takes away something precious, the ocean tells me, He sends another gift in its place. —ELIZABETH SHERRILL

> *Father, I have lost my friend. What new avenue of love*
> *will You open to me today?*

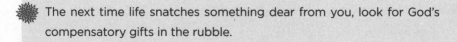 The next time life snatches something dear from you, look for God's compensatory gifts in the rubble.

ENDURING PRESENCE

But as for me, it is good to be near God.... —PSALM 73:28 (NIV)

MY FRIEND BRENT LIVES NEXT DOOR AND WAS KNOWN THROUGHOUT OUR neighborhood as a mild-mannered, quiet, thoughtful person. This all came to an abrupt end one morning when he watched his only daughter suffer a terrible tragedy. I don't even want to reveal what that tragedy was, but suffice it to say that Brent's daughter was hurt more than any teenager should ever be—and Brent was furious with God.

It was shocking to see. Sitting in his living room, Brent explained bitterly, "The deal is over. God is supposed to love us, and I don't see any love left." He was mad, but his anger masked a very deep sadness and sense of loss.

God, guide me, I thought. I had no idea what to say in this situation, even though I had read the books and articles and heard the sermons that explained how God is love and is ready and waiting to love us, even, and especially, when awful things happen. My friend already knew all of that anyway.

I felt like I shouldn't say anything. And so, I just listened…and listened for the better part of a year. At the end of that year, I began to see Brent's daughter heal. And just when I was about to suggest to Brent what I'd wanted to suggest earlier—that God is good and wants all that is good for us even though this world often offers up what is painful—he beat me to it.

Today, Brent and his daughter and God are all back on the same page. Of course, they always were. —JON SWEENEY

I praise You, God, for Your enduring presence,
even when I am angry or frustrated with You.

When a friend or acquaintance experiences an unspeakable loss, sit with them and hear their story.

MORNING IS COMING

And there followed him a great company of people, and of women, which also bewailed and lamented him. But Jesus turning unto them said, Daughters of Jerusalem, weep not for me.... —LUKE 23:27–28 (KJV)

MY SISTER CINDY DIED THREE YEARS AGO, AND I HAVE YET TO CRY. I'VE cried about other tragedies, other deaths, but not about my sister.

"Strange" does not begin to describe this behavior. Cindy was quadriplegic—had been for forty-five-plus years. I could say she suffered (she did); I can say her death was a release (it was); I can even say the clichés: "She was needed in heaven" (I wouldn't know). But I couldn't explain my dry-eyed grieving.

Late one night, my ever-patient wife said, "You know, you already mourned your sister." I assumed Sandee wanted to start a large fight with a large insult. I hadn't even *begun* to mourn. Then she added, "You mourned when she was alive. You celebrated who she had become, but you mourned the loss. You mourned that Cindy couldn't walk. You mourned that she was in pain. It's okay. You were a good brother. You *are* a good brother."

This revelation was Sandee's gift to me. No one can tell you when to cry. Grief follows its own etiquette; death is rude; it lacks dignity, tramples timetables.

I doubt Jesus's gentle admonishment to the daughters of Jerusalem worked (Do you really think they stopped crying?), but now I get the point: It's okay to mourn and it's okay to finish mourning because morning is coming. —MARK COLLINS

Lord, Your death overcame sin but did not overcome sadness.
Teach us how to grieve our losses as we celebrate Your victory. Amen.

 Take a moment to acknowledge the sadness in your heart. Ask God to help you let it go.

PRAISE THE LORD EVERY DAY

Let every thing that hath breath praise the Lord. Praise ye the Lord.
—Psalm 150:6 (KJV)

A FRIEND WAS GRIEVING THE DEATH OF HER MOTHER. AN OBSERVANT JEW, she was saying the *kaddish* prayer, the traditional Jewish prayer of mourning.

"Is it something you just pray at home?" I asked.

"On the contrary," she said. "You're only supposed to say the mourners' kaddish in community." Every morning on her way to work, she stops by her synagogue to gather with a small group who say this ancient prayer together.

"Why in a group?" I asked. "Wouldn't it be easier to say it on your own?"

"That's one of the important principles of saying *kaddish*. If you're grieving, you should be with others. You shouldn't be alone."

"What are the words of the prayer?" I assumed the language would be something like Lamentations, full of chest-pounding agony. "It must be comforting to express your sorrow in a group."

"The words aren't about sorrow or loss," she explained. "They're full of praise." She quoted the opening text, inspired by Ezekiel 38:23: "May his great name be blessed forever and to all eternity."

"How long do you do this?" I asked.

"For a year."

A year of praise during a year of grieving. I thought of those times I struggled over loss and how an uplifting song could pull me out of myself. Here it was, a spiritual practice that demonstrated the same healing truth. —RICK HAMLIN

Today and every day, I praise You, O Lord!

 Remember someone you've lost. Praise God for the precious memories you have of her or him.

HE OPENS THE HEAVENS

For great is your love, higher than the heavens; your faithfulness reaches to the skies. —PSALM 108:4 (NIV)

PLUMES OF WHITE MIST HOVERED OVER THE BUBBLING WATER AS I SAT IN our hot tub on a frigid night. The sky was intensely black, a perfect backdrop for a universe of dazzling pinpoints of light. I took a deep breath and released it slowly, wishing the soothing water would absorb the depth of loss I felt.

I missed my mother terribly. It had been about one month since she had died at the age of ninety-four. She had lived a long and vibrant life, full of appreciation for God's wonders, which she often described as "exquisite!" How she would have loved this night.

"Mother," I said out loud, "are you out there somewhere?"

Even if she is, I thought, *her brightness would be eclipsed by tonight's radiant stars.*

That thought had barely formed when the largest, most brilliant, most magnificent comet I have ever seen streaked across the sky and then fizzled out as quickly as it had come.

An intense joy filled me. I laughed out loud. I clapped. I knew without a doubt that all was well with my mother. I could almost hear her say, "Wasn't that exquisite?" —KIM HENRY

Thank You, Lord God, that out of Your goodness and Your love,
You even open up the heavens to us.

Is there someone you're desperately missing today? Emulate a favorite attribute of theirs.

Dear Lord, guide me to believe fully in the sun when it is concealed behind the clouds, the earth when it is covered in asphalt, the rainbow before the rain ends, and You in every living thing. Even if You seem hidden, let me always believe that You are there.

RHODA BLECKER

Chapter 7

WHEN YOU FEEL LONELY

....

Humans may be social beings, but solitude has been shown to have great societal value. Jesus was a great healer and teacher, but He took time to rest and pray. Solitude is essential for our spiritual experience—it is where we hear the still, small voice.

FROM *RENEWED: FINDING YOUR INNER HAPPY IN AN OVERWHELMED WORLD* BY LUCILLE ZIMMERMAN

SPEAK WORDS OF CHEER

Kind words are like honey—enjoyable and healthful. —PROVERBS 16:24 (TLB)

SEVERAL YEARS AGO I WAS CAR SHOPPING VIA THE NEWSPAPER CLASSIFIEDS when a black-bordered display ad caught my attention.

> TOMORROW IS MY 60TH BIRTHDAY.
> I LIVE ALONE AND WOULD
> LOVE TO CELEBRATE WITH
> CALLS FROM PEOPLE OF ALL AGES.

I cut out the notice. I prayed that the woman would have a happy birthday and receive lots of nice calls. I picked up the telephone three times. But I didn't dial the number to say, "Happy Birthday!"

I had occasion to remember that ad on my birthday last year. Why? Because only my daughter Rebecca wished me a happy day. My husband Don's mid-morning e-mail to my office didn't count. "Sorry I forgot your birthday," it read, "but I got you a card." Translated (as only someone married forty-plus years can do), that meant he'd made a quick trip to the dollar store.

At sixty-plus I'm old enough to understand that forgetting my birthday is trivial compared to the love and kindness with which my family and friends typically surround me. I hope I'm also old enough to understand that every opportunity to brighten another person's day is a gift from God.

—PENNEY SCHWAB

Lord, next time—every time—give me the courage and courtesy
to speak words of love and cheer to one of Your lonely children.

Ask God to bring to mind someone who is isolated from the outside world. Take them a small treat.

THE JOY OF ANIMAL FRIENDS

Praise be to the God and Father of our Lord Jesus Christ, the Father of compassion and the God of all comfort. —2 CORINTHIANS 1:3 (NIV)

WALLY IS A MEDIUM-SIZED DOG WITH A WOOLLY BROWN COAT AND A PAIR of the warmest, sweetest eyes imaginable. He wears a colored scarf around his neck, identifying him as a "Good Dog" who has been trained and licensed by the Good Dog Foundation to interact with the sick. His handler, Irene, has also taken the eleven weeks of training that assures each Good Dog has a special way of engaging with strangers in an unfamiliar environment.

Wally is amazing. I watch with fascination as he trots to the bedside of a frail and barely conscious hospice patient named Anne. She reaches out her open hand, and Wally lifts up his front paw, puts it into her hand, and moves his head to be stroked.

All over the country there are more than one thousand Good Dogs doing good work for the lonely and the sick. The sight of Wally as he wags his tail and enters another room immediately reminds me of the hymn: "All creatures great and small, All things wise and wonderful: The Lord God made them all."

God definitely had a hand in creating Wally, the Good Dog.

—BRIGITTE WEEKS

Let us give thanks and praise, God, for all our animal friends and the solace they bring.

When you spot a neighbor with their beloved pet, thank them for the joy they bring the neighborhood.

WILLING TO SEE

"Serve Him with a loyal heart and with a willing mind...."
—1 Chronicles 28:9 (nkjv)

The six-week-old golden retriever puppies wiggled at my feet, chewing on my shoelaces and tackling one another on the lawn. They were so cute, I wanted them all. *Lord,* I prayed, *help me choose the right one.*

I had already paid a deposit, but I couldn't decide which one I wanted. Then I discovered *The Art of Raising a Puppy,* which had a puppy test to help in making a choice. It said separate each puppy from its siblings and mother, put it through some simple exercises, and match its responses to the ones in the book. Each response earned points that indicated a particular canine personality. To keep track of each puppy, I stuck a colored star on its head.

I scooped up Red Star, set her down a hundred yards away, and called her. She ran to me with her tail up, and I checked response number three. Systematically I scored each pup. One wasn't even interested in the test, but the others had the same score, except Green Star.

When I crouched down beside her and waved a puppy-sized cloth dummy in front of her face and then tossed it, she chased it and pounced. She lay down and chewed on the end, then suddenly lifted her head and looked at me as if to say, "Oh, I forgot something." She stood up, grabbed the dummy, and brought it to me, setting it down in my hand. I reached down and ruffled her fur.

I didn't have to total up Green Star's score; I knew I was in love.
—Rebecca Ondov

> *Lord, like the puppy You chose for me,*
> *let me have a willing heart.*

 First thing tomorrow morning, say a big "yes" to God. In fact, start now!

ISOLATING TIMES

Let us therefore no longer pass judgment on one another....
—ROMANS 14:13 (NRSV)

FRIENDS OF MINE WERE TALKING ABOUT THE JOYS AND AGGRAVATIONS OF our families. Abruptly one said, "Sometimes I feel so isolated, even within my family. Maybe that's just the way life is these days—people feel alone."

The lighthearted banter stopped. It wasn't that we pitied her; it was that, at some level, each of us understood. She recalled how she and her brother had tried family therapy. She'd always thought he was perfect. During the sessions, he spoke about his terrific life, his perfect wife, children, job. My friend had felt inadequate. At their last session, she believed the therapy had been a waste of time. On their way to the parking lot, her brother said, "I never feel like I'm really part of things. I feel like I've always been alone."

How easily we misperceive others, especially those close to us. For decades, my friend had considered her brother too high and mighty to bother with her, much less to have the same problems she had. I do the same thing. I consider my husband too affable and well-adjusted to ever be hurt until I say something careless to him. I think of my neighbor as the perfect Christian and then she tells me she's stopped going to church. I label my friend Jeff as the world's most solicitous son, only to have him confess he's not speaking to his parents.

Maybe we live in lonely times, but perhaps that is because of our unwillingness to try to understand the person beside us. —MARCI ALBORGHETTI

Holy Spirit, imbue me with a desire to learn
about those around me.

Reach out to someone who is living alone. Let her or him know you're there.

KEEPING IN TOUCH

Therefore encourage one another with these words. —1 THESSALONIANS 4:18 (NIV)

"IT TOOK ME THIRTY MINUTES TO WRITE YOU THAT TEXT MESSAGE YESTERDAY," Dad said.

I wasn't sure I'd heard him correctly over the phone. "Thirty minutes?" I asked.

"Yes."

"It was only two sentences long."

"Well, I am kind of new to this technology."

We both laughed.

Dad was new to cell phones; he and Mom had shared a mobile phone for a couple of years, but it was only for emergencies. Dad finally got his own phone last year, around the same time I moved from our home state of Virginia to California for graduate school.

I don't know how I would have gotten through those difficult days when I first arrived at school had it not been for the communication with my family that modern technology afforded me. Whenever I felt lonely or frustrated, I'd call or e-mail Mom or Dad, and they always had something encouraging to say.

I thank God that I live in an age when I can build relationships with my family no matter where my travels take me—and that it no longer takes Dad thirty minutes to reply to my text messages. —JOSHUA SUNDQUIST

Thank You, Lord, for the people You've put in my life and
for the means You've given us to keep in touch.

Create a scrapbook. Fill it with pictures and mementos of good friends. Let them know about it to help you fill it and share the connection.

THE GIFT OF SOLITUDE

Then they were glad because they had quiet, and he brought them to their desired haven. —PSALM 107:30 (RSV)

I AM TOTALLY ALONE THIS WEEKEND. MY HUSBAND AND SON WENT TO A barbershop chorus convention, and my daughter is away with her best friend's family. That leaves me and our dog—and I must admit I'm enjoying it. I love my family, yet there's something refreshing about making my own schedule (or no schedule, if I choose), having cereal for dinner, and watching *Field of Dreams* two nights in a row (and crying shamelessly both times).

When I told a friend about how I planned to spend the weekend, she said, "Won't you get lonely?" I wondered why I hadn't thought about that, and then I ran across this quote from an unknown author: "The difference between loneliness and solitude is how you feel about who you are alone with and who made the choice."

I feel good about who I'm with because it really isn't just me. These times of solitude provide my very best times with God. In fact, on my rare weekends alone, it feels as if God has made this choice for me, a gift of quiet time so that I will give some back to Him. When I do, I realize that solitude is one of God's best presents, especially in a world that is too busy, too noisy, and too crowded. Free of demands and distractions, I sit with my Bible on the back porch swing and rest with God. In the quiet peace that follows, God teaches me that loneliness is simply a space into which He has not yet been invited. —GINA BRIDEGMAN

Lord Jesus, come sit beside me when I am alone;
I want to spend time with You.

Carve out a period of solitude and commit to it on your calendar as if it were an engagement with a treasured friend. It is.

ALL IN GOOD TIME

And, lo, I am with you always, even unto the end of the world....
—MATTHEW 28:20 (KJV)

I LIKE SURPRISES, LITTLE UNEXPECTED THINGS THAT PICK ME UP ON A LONELY or difficult day. When I get home, I always look in the mailbox before opening the front door. I'm eager to know if I've received a letter from a friend. I'm thrilled when my hopes are fulfilled and disappointed when only bills greet me.

When I work at my computer, I fight the urge to pause and check my e-mail. I want to find out if someone has reached across the expanse of cyberspace to contact me, to say hello, ask a question, share a thought.

This same thing is true in my spiritual life. I long to feel the presence of God. I often open my Bible seeking a "letter from God," a special word addressed to me. Early in the morning or late at night, I take long walks and talk aloud to my Creator. Many times it's a monologue, and I can only hear the sound of my own voice. But occasionally the monologue is transformed into a dialogue. I hear no heavenly voice, but I know that God is talking to me. And when that happens, it's a joyous surprise.

And so I guess I have a choice: I can sit and wait for others to communicate, or I can take the initiative and write the letter, flash the smile, give the gift, or share the touch. Above all, I can faithfully talk to God, knowing that in His own good time He will speak to me. —SCOTT WALKER

Father, in the midst of loneliness, may I remember the words of
Saint Francis: "For it is in giving that we receive." Amen.

Is there a neighbor whom folks tend to ignore? Bake them a cake using an old family recipe.

KINDNESS IN THE LITTLE THINGS

*God sets the lonely in families.... —*PSALM 68:6 (NIV)

EVERY CHRISTMAS SOMEONE FROM OUR CHURCH FAMILY HOSTS A PARTY for our pastor, staff members, and members of the church council. Last year my wife and I participated in the white elephant gift exchange. Each person draws a number and chooses a gift. (Maybe the word *gift* is a little misleading. The paper it's wrapped in is often worth more than the present itself.)

I drew a low number and unwrapped a Chia Pet, a present that doubtlessly disappointed its recipient and would have been discarded had white elephants not been invented as a way of recycling useless objects like Chia Pets.

One of the rules of our gift exchange is that every participant can choose a wrapped package or "steal" something someone else has unwrapped. Nobody was interested in stealing my Chia Pet. A desperate thief with very poor taste would not steal a Chia Pet. "It's better than a pet rock," I said, hoping to pique someone's interest, but it was no use. I was left out of the game completely. To my surprise I discovered that being left out is just as painful at fifty-four as it is at fourteen.

After about a half hour of being ignored, a Good Samaritan snubbed all the other gifts and seized my Chia Pet as if he had longed for it all his life. And you know, I discovered that there's no age limit to feeling grateful for an unexpected kindness either; it's just as wonderful at fifty-four as it is at fourteen. —TIM WILLIAMS

Dear God, thank You for the special people who
place kindness above competition.

Extend an unexpected kindness to someone who absolutely doesn't deserve it.

THE RICHNESS OF LOVE

Inasmuch as ye have done it unto one of the least of these my brethren, ye have done it unto me. —MATTHEW 25:40 (KJV)

WE WANTED A DONKEY TO HELP WARD OFF COYOTES ON OUR FAMILY RANCH. Word got around, and a man contacted us with a real deal. Mr. Hyde was free and delivered, so we agreed. How could we go wrong? However, one look at the ancient donkey and we knew he wasn't up to the task. We'd keep him anyway. We were appalled when the previous owner claimed he'd used him for roping practice. Mr. Hyde was shaggy, thin, and obviously neglected.

His gentle demeanor was partially masked by his overwhelming shyness. It was apparent he'd known love previously in his life, but that was ages ago and he'd long since given up expecting to see it ever again.

My heart went out to the lonely donkey. "Lord, let him remember love," I whispered.

We kept Mr. Hyde near the ranch house with heifers for company. At first I could barely approach him, even with alfalfa hay. He'd tense up or walk away when I tried to pet him. Gradually, he started to trust me. The first time he followed me home, I could barely contain my elation. Now when he sees me, he comes up to me for attention and nuzzles my hands for treats. In his eyes, I'm starting to see the love returned to me. —ERIKA BENTSEN

Dear Lord, thank You for showing me it's better to give love, even when it doesn't seem to matter. The richness of love in return is above all earthly value!

> If you have a coworker who has long since given up expecting friendship, ask them to join your group for lunch.

EMBRACING THOSE SHUT OUT

Grace to you and peace. —1 Thessalonians 1:1 (RSV)

At first, I thought he was a construction worker on a lunch break. He was sitting on the curb, with food almost gone from a plastic plate. But as our eyes met, he asked, "Spare change?" I dug in my purse and hurriedly gave him a few coins; I was on my own lunch break.

About to leave, I was startled when he patted the curb. "Sit a minute, please." I did, and he said, "They kicked me out of there." He pointed toward a fast-food place down the street. "I picked up a plate or two that people had left, and they told me to get out." I was horrified. He continued: "People in a church I used to go to always used to worry about shut-ins. But what about us shut-outs?"

Dear God, what have I gotten into here?

I wondered what it would be like to be kicked out of a fast-food restaurant, and thought of several times in my life I'd felt shut out: from being last to be chosen for a team and even being disowned by a relative. It's a lonely, isolating feeling.

Still…I've got to go back to work, I thought, torn.

Then he stuck his hand out. "I'm Kevin."

I shook his hand. "I'm Linda," I said.

"Thanks for shaking my hand, Linda," Kevin said. "You're probably in a rush," he said. "Everyone is."

I started to rise and then stopped. "I have a little time," I said. "Work can wait." —Linda Neukrug

> Lord, today let me not exclude another human being from
> my circle. After all, You don't shut anybody out.

Reflect on a time when *you* felt left out. What helped you feel included? Look for an opportunity to emulate that behavior.

COURAGE FOR THE INTROVERT

All discipline for the moment seems not to be joyful, but sorrowful; yet to those who have been trained by it, afterwards it yields the peaceful fruit of righteousness. —HEBREWS 12:11 (NAS)

I GET WHAT DAVID MURROW TALKS ABOUT IN HIS BOOK *WHY MEN HATE Going to Church*. I don't hate church, but it's more discipline than delight.

For one thing, I am terribly restless. In church, I feel like a racehorse confined to a broom closet. Sitting on a hard chair for an hour of Sunday school and an hour of worship stretches me to the edge of sanity. And when I am forced to be very quiet, I become overly aware of my minor maladies. My acid reflux begins to burn like a blowtorch. The tickle in my throat becomes a raging itch. I cough uncontrollably until my wife pokes me. "*Shh*, people are staring."

Last, I am an introvert and I get claustrophobic with people sitting on all sides of me. Church isn't easy. It's a discipline, like going to the doctor.

What brings me back is the payoff. I feel less lonely for having seen all my fellow-strugglers in the same place, looking for help. I make better decisions at work because my conscience has been sharpened by good preaching. And when I walk out the front door of the church, I feel fifty pounds lighter because I have left my sins in the hands of a merciful God.

It's worth the discomfort, I think. —DANIEL SCHANTZ

Lord, You are the Great Physician. I don't like going to doctors and I chafe at going to church, but I thank You for the healing I experience every Sunday.

If there's something you dread doing, try to find a small nugget of joy or satisfaction in it.

EMBRACING THE POSSIBILITIES

Joy cometh in the morning. —Psalm 30:5 (kjv)

It is early morning as I make my way through the unlit house, moving toward the smell of fresh brewing coffee. I have always liked the quiet dark before daybreak.

In the kitchen, the air is chilly, telling me that I missed closing the window the night before. Now, through the opened window, I hear a lone bird singing: "*Purdy…purdy…purdy…*" It fills the kitchen, so I sit down and listen. And then a second sound: "*What-cheer…what-cheer…what-cheer…*" And a third: "*Chewick…chewick…*" Soon there's a symphony of birdsong greeting the dawn!

Later, as I go full throttle into the day, I think of the bird who led the way, how he sang because he could, how the other birds followed. Stopping by the shoe shop, I dash in to pick up my favorite clogs. I notice the smell of leather and polish and the sound of a sewing machine whirring. Somehow, the shop seems beautiful. I call out to the repairman, "I want you to know how much I appreciate your work! These are the most comfortable shoes imaginable…and you've given them new life."

A smile spreads across his face. And as I leave the shop, I hear a second customer adding, "You know, she's right. You do a mighty good job."

That night, I was careful to leave the window open to whatever possibilities a new day might offer. If one lone bird can claim the moment with his optimistic song, then surely I can find a way to do the same. —Pam Kidd

Father, I don't want to skim over the days You give me. Help me to listen, to live deeply, and to give with great joy.

Be like the birds of the air today. Lead the way with a joyous song. Just because you can.

OUR HOPE FOR EACH NEW DAY

Lord, thou hast been our dwelling place in all generations. Before the mountains were brought forth, or ever thou hadst formed the earth and the world, even from everlasting to everlasting, thou art God. —PSALM 90:1–2 (KJV)

IT'S NEW YEAR'S EVE. MY WIFE, BETH, IS ACCOMPANYING TWELVE BAYLOR University students on a study abroad program in Hong Kong, Cambodia, Vietnam, Singapore, and Thailand. My oldest son, Drew, and his fiancée are traveling in India. My youngest son, Luke, is teaching English in Bangkok. And my daughter, Jodi, is driving from Texas to school in South Carolina. I'm at home in Waco with four golden retrievers to bring in the new year.

With my family scattered all over the world, I'm lonely. Worrying about my family's safety has my anxiety level up. Like so many on the threshold of a new year, I face change in my life and the dawning awareness that a chapter of life is closing for good. In an uncertain world, I yearn for stability.

I find myself spontaneously humming a tune. It's a hymn, with words written by Isaac Watts three hundred years ago. I know of no better hymn to sing to bring us through the promise and the challenge of the coming year.

O God, our help in ages past,
Our hope for years to come,
Our shelter from the stormy blast,
And our eternal home. —SCOTT WALKER

Father, You have been through every year of my life to sustain me and supply my needs. Stay by my side as my loving Shepherd as we walk through this new year together.

When a chapter of *your* life is closing, before moving on, thank the folks who have helped you.

INCLUDING THE LONELY

*God setteth the solitary in families.... —*PSALM 68:6 (KJV)

WHEN I WAS A TODDLER, THE PEOPLE WHO FILLED OUR DINING ROOM, wearing pointy hats and singing "Happy Birthday," included an interesting collection of folks who might have otherwise spent the day alone: widows, widowers, or never-been-marrieds. As I grew older, I remember enviously attending friends' celebrations and laying it on thick: "Aw, Mom, Jimmy had Madame Fee-fee, the gypsy magician, at his birthday!"

My mom had the perfect rebuttal: "Yes, Brock, but when you share your special day with people who love you as much as the 'old people' do, you get a present that lasts forever and it's better than anything money can buy."

Now, as my fortieth birthday approaches, I find myself thinking of those parties and those dear "old people," most of whom have died. I think about greeting Mae Davis at the door as my father folded up her walker and helped her to the couch. I remember Louise, Kathleen, Walter, and Gordon sitting around the table, cheering as I blew out the candles. And there was always Kate; never married and no family of her own, she was adopted into our family early on.

All these years later, the present my mother alluded to is a very real part of who I am. It might have been a challenging lesson for a ten-year-old boy, but it is a powerfully pertinent one to a soon-to-be-forty-year-old man.

On the morning of my fortieth, I made a phone call. "Hey, Mom, how about meeting me at the nursing home for a mini-celebration before my birthday dinner? I can't imagine my special day without a visit with Kate." —BROCK KIDD

Father, keep me mindful to open my home and
my heart to Your lonely children.

 Make a plan to celebrate your special day in a new way this year!

MISSING A LOVED ONE

But if any widow has children or grandchildren, let them first learn to show piety at home and to repay their parents; for this is good and acceptable before God.
—1 TIMOTHY 5:4 (NKJV)

EVEN THOUGH IT WAS ONE OF THOSE GORGEOUS DAYS IN FLORIDA, I WAS feeling lonely and left out because it was my son Michael's thirty-seventh birthday and he was a thousand miles away in Cincinnati, Ohio.

I missed all four of my children and their families, scattered in California, Wisconsin, and Ohio. I was feeling envious of my snowbird friends who only come to Florida for the winter and then return north to be near their families.

I'd left two messages on Michael's home phone and his cell phone. *Where is he?* I'd sung "Happy Birthday"—twice—and I wanted to talk to my son!

Late that night, I checked my messages and there was a long, over-the-top-happy message from Michael. "Mom, it's been a great day! We all went to church. Then Amy and the kids took me out to brunch and then home, where I opened gifts. Thanks for the shirts and the tie—they're terrific! Then I got to play golf with a good friend all afternoon on a perfect, gorgeous day. Right now I'm relaxing in my hammock, Amy's baking my birthday cake, the pizza's on its way, and later I'm going to go play basketball. Mom, sometimes I feel like an old man, but my wonderful wife and kids made this such an extra-special day for me that I can't complain. I even loved your singing. Call me! I love you!"

I couldn't have topped that day for my son. I didn't get to hug him in person, but that phone call sure made me feel like a hug. —PATRICIA LORENZ

Lord, help me to treasure every phone call, e-mail, letter, and visit with my kids and to be grateful they're all happy.

If you are missing your children, call them and tell them so.

BOOKS OPEN UP THE WORLD

Write the vision, and make it plain upon tables, that he may run that readeth it.
—HABAKKUK 2:2 (KJV)

ANNA KARENINA IS A BIG BOOK—840 PAGES IN MY HARDCOVER EDITION—
and it weighs a couple of pounds. It's a lot to lug around, but the best opportunity
I have for reading is going from place to place. So I took Tolstoy's novel everywhere
with me. I read it on the subway and the bus. I read it on the treadmill at the gym.
I confess I even read it while walking to work (without bumping into anyone).

But when I wasn't reading it, the characters were still with me. There was a
dark-haired woman who looked just like Anna coming out of Lord and Taylor.
The dashing Vronsky strolled right out of a brokerage on Fifth Avenue, walking down the avenue like he owned the place. At the farmer's market in Union
Square, I was sure I spotted the earnest farmer Levin. He wore a floppy leather
hat, a bemused expression, and he was carrying a bag of corn.

And then there were all the people I met who were great fans of the book.
One man stopped me on the street and asked, "How do you like it?" Another
time, I was reading the novel on the bus when I heard a woman's voice, "Where
are you?" I looked up. "Has Levin proposed to Kitty yet?" she asked.

"He's proposed once," I said, "but I'm waiting for him to do it again."

Many would say that reading a book is a solitary activity. Perhaps, but I
don't think a reader can ever be lonely. The best books—whether it's Tolstoy or
the Bible—open us up to a whole new world. Especially on the streets of New
York City. —RICK HAMLIN

I give thanks for the world of books, Lord.

 Books are a great conversation starter. If you aren't already in a book
club, consider joining one, or starting one at your church.

NOURISHED THROUGH FRIENDSHIP

They shall feed every one in his place. —JEREMIAH 6:3 (KJV)

PHYLLIS, MY NEXT-DOOR NEIGHBOR'S MOTHER, ALWAYS WORE AN APRON. That's because she was always cooking: rolling out piecrusts for the firefighters in her picturesque New Hampshire town, shaping dozens of her famous mountain cookies for bake sales, or simmering Boston baked beans for church suppers. If food was needed, Phyllis was there. When her daughter Janice invited me over for cookouts, supposedly Phyllis's day off, I'd enjoy the conversation—and Phyllis's creamy potato salad with a yummy extra something. That woman just *had* to cook.

Now Phyllis knew that I felt lonely living on the lake in the winter, especially during that first empty-nest year following my daughter Trina's graduation. So during the darkest evenings of the year, Phyllis included me at her table for a proper Sunday dinner: meat, potatoes, gravy, several vegetables, and two desserts, a true labor of love whipped up by a woman nearly eighty years old and too diabetic to eat most of it. Yet how she nourished so many of us!

Then one July afternoon, God suddenly called Phyllis home. Janice found her mother near the door of the sun porch, wearing her apron. In her hand Phyllis held bread; she had been on her way to feed the birds.
—GAIL THORELL SCHILLING

Lord, thank You for the ways dear Phyllis nourished me.
Use me to carry on her pantry ministry.

 Invite a friend to a spur-of-the-moment grab-bag lunch.

A SMILE IS THE BEST WELCOME

May we...lift up our banners in the name of our God.... —PSALM 20:5 (NIV)

WHEN OUR SON CHRIS WAS DUE BACK IN NORTH CAROLINA AFTER HIS fifteen-month deployment to Iraq, my husband, Gordon, ordered an eight-foot-long, bright green plastic banner that said, "Welcome Home, Capt. Chris Barber!" On arrival day Gordon nailed the banner to two eight-foot poles. When he and our son John lifted it up, I thought, *That's way too big.*

As we crowded behind a rope outside the hangar at the airfield, the banner was so big that Gordon had to stand at the back of the crowd. I stood up front and cheered as our soldiers came down the aircraft steps. Suddenly, they began marching quickly toward doors. Families crammed through a single doorway; I couldn't see Gordon.

I was barely in the door when a loudspeaker began playing "The Star-Spangled Banner." I froze in place and put my hand over my heart, feeling lost. I'd felt lonely with my son so far away. And now I couldn't get to him. Two teardrops fell onto my hand. How would I ever find my family in the chaos when the ropes separating us from the soldiers were undone?

Suddenly something big and green caught my eye: the impossibly big banner! By the time I reached it, Chris had found it too. We hugged and smiled.

As we left the hangar, it occurred to me that you can never really go overboard on signs of love. Lift up your banner high today so that those who are feeling lost and lonely can gladly gather 'round! —KAREN BARBER

Dear Father, make my smile a banner that
welcomes everyone home to Your love.

 Remember things that make you smile. Share those thoughts to encourage someone to smile.

SHEDDING YOUR OLD SELF

He found him in a desert land, and in the waste howling wilderness; he led him about, he instructed him, he kept him as the apple of his eye. —Deuteronomy 32:10 (KJV)

At some point—let's say 4:37 am—the phone will ring; it won't be a wrong number. Or maybe it'll be a knock on the door. The receptionist will say, "The doctor will see you now." A baby will arrive. Or your daughter will wed and you'll be crying. It'll happen. And for the millionth time you'll muster your resources: family, friends, people...until one day when they won't.

For some sudden reason you're alone. Who knows why? But the folks you counted on aren't there. No malice aforethought; they just couldn't make it.

You're alone, utterly. But you're not utterly alone. Every prophet, every pauper has taken this journey—forty days in the desert or forty years.

But that's not the end of it. All of these lonely, painful journeys share something else: shedding your old self. Not only shedding the usual suspects (possessions, prepossessions, presumptions), but shedding your old way of thinking. Maybe your friends didn't abandon you; maybe they're on their own journey and you were too tired to lift your head to notice. Maybe you think you cannot soldier on. Yet here you are, reading this, soldiering on.

Maybe that's where you find God—in this new life that has emerged unasked, against all odds. Maybe that's grace, showing up at 4:53 am, carrying solace and holiness and redemption like a small, precious child. —Mark Collins

Lord, I see You now, tracing my wayward tracks through
the desert. And now that the dust has settled in front of me,
I have some idea of where I'm going. Against all odds. Amen.

 Take inventory of the little reminders (photos, old cards) that say you are loved.

SPREADING GOODWILL

Two are better than one, because they have a good return for their labor: if either of them falls down, one can help the other up. But pity anyone who falls and has no one to help them up. —ECCLESIASTES 4:9–10 (NIV)

FOR A COUNTRY GIRL, BEING IN A LARGE CITY AWAY FROM HOME AT CHRISTMAS was unnerving. For days I fought the traffic in department stores, trying to find a present for my mother, but nothing was affordable.

"Why don't you hold a promotional party?" a coworker suggested. "If you get enough sales, you get a lace tablecloth." *A perfect gift!* I thought.

But who would come? Being new in the city, I didn't know many people. Still, I had to try. I wrote a guest list and made arrangements with the company.

On the appointed day a saleswoman entered my studio, decorated with cedar boughs and red candles. She spread her wares across my bed and then we waited for the guests to arrive. None came.

Promptly at 7:30 PM, Lily, my landlady, arrived. "Where is everybody?" she asked and then hurried out of the room.

"I suppose we should call it off," the saleswoman said.

Suddenly there was a noise at the door, and two women entered. "Hi. We live down the street. Lily tells us there's a party here," they said. Bewildered, I asked them to sit down. This scenario repeated itself until the room filled with new faces. Then Lily herself entered, winked, and sat down.

Yes, I did receive the coveted tablecloth—and so much more.

—HELEN GRACE LESCHEID

Father, help me to spread goodwill to all who are lonely.

 Visit a friend or relative who is shut in. Remind them they are not alone.

WINGS AND ROOTS

A wise son maketh a glad father.... —PROVERBS 10:1 (KJV)

A FRIEND OF MINE CLAIMS THAT IT'S THE JOB OF A PARENT TO GIVE A CHILD roots and wings. Well, when Timothy went to college and Carol and I no longer had any boys at home, I was worried that maybe we'd overdone it with the wings. Our house was too quiet without them. I felt lonely without them.

I mean, for the first week Tim didn't even call, and after that we'd get only nuggets: He loved his classes, he had great friends, he was playing Frisbee on the lawn and working hard. But in my empty-nest stage, I kept wondering: Didn't he miss us? Didn't he miss our fall rituals, like shopping for apples at the green market, going to a Columbia football game, carving a jack-o'-lantern, planting the spring bulbs? Every November we'd put in tulip bulbs and daffodils and crocuses. Now I'd have to do it on my own. A lonely task now.

"I'm glad Tim's happy," I'd pray, "but fall feels empty without him."

Then one day I came home from work and Carol said, "There's a package for you on the dining room table." A sizable cardboard box from some unknown address. I opened it. On top was a card. "Happy Father's Day a little late," it said. "Love, Tim." In the box were spring bulbs to plant in the autumn.

"What a great present, Tim!" I told him on the phone. "I'm glad you didn't forget."

"Sure, Dad," he said.

Wings and roots: It takes both. —RICK HAMLIN

Lord, may my children remember where they're from
as they spread their wings and fly.

Look at your kids' photo albums. Relish the memories made and those yet to come.

"YOU CAME BELIEVING"

I believe that I shall see the goodness of the Lord in the land of the living!
—Psalm 27:13 (RSV)

A LONE TRAVELER IN PARIS, I WAS LIVING A DREAM, A BIRTHDAY PRESENT
from my mother and stepfather. For years I'd longed to test my wings and
travel alone. This was it. I could walk for miles, stopping whenever I wanted to
take photos. When it rained, I wrapped my camera in plastic and walked on.
I lingered in ancient cemeteries searching out marble angels, and no one said,
"Hurry!" There were no schedules—just me, my camera, a tiny hotel room a
block from the Eiffel Tower, and a city to explore.

The time went quickly. It was my last day—my *Mona Lisa* day. "Small,
dark, disappointing," I'd heard people say about it, but I was undaunted.

I trekked along the Seine toward the Louvre and found a crowd waiting to
get in. "It's Free Day," someone explained. "Half of Paris is here."

Oops. I circled back and sat down to think. I remembered reading that the
Louvre had a back entrance. *Worth a try*, I thought.

Soon I was chatting with the guard at the back door. He was young and
sweet and liked my Southern accent. I was in!

I walked through the exhibits until I stood before her, transfixed. She was familiar, like a good friend. And why not? She'd been an image in my head practically
all my life. My eyes filled with tears. I looked at the guard. "She's beautiful," I said.

"Ah," he said, "you came believing. Yes?" —PAM KIDD

Father, wherever I go in life, believing makes all the difference.
Open my eyes and let me see the best Your world offers.

Step out of your comfort zone today. Don't let the fact that you are
alone deter you from experiencing something beautiful.

Thank You for Your tender mercies, thank You for Your desire that we be whole, thank You for the angels You sent through the people who helped me become strong again.

....

Jacki Keck

Chapter 8

WHEN YOU NEED GUIDANCE

....

Some changes look negative on the surface but you will soon realize that space is being created in your life for something new to emerge.

ECKHART TOLLE

GOD'S GREAT COUNSEL

"Choose my instruction instead of silver, knowledge rather than choice gold, for wisdom is more precious than rubies, and nothing you desire can compare with her." —PROVERBS 8:10–11 (NIV)

A FEW YEARS AGO I RECEIVED AN E-MAIL TELLING ME THAT THE WHITE House was considering me for a presidential appointment as a national advocate for volunteerism. *Wow*, I thought, *this is so exciting!* I figured the interview would be a breeze because I had been volunteering for many years.

But during the interview, such simple questions as "Can you please list the volunteer positions you've held?" and "Why do you care about volunteerism?" left me struggling for words. Needless to say, I wasn't selected for the position.

Soon after, I asked my dad what he thought went wrong.

"Did you prepare?" he asked.

"A little," I said.

"Well, when I have a job interview, I try to prepare as much as possible. In fact, I try to overprepare."

I took his words to heart. Last year I applied for a position cohosting an Internet TV show in Los Angeles. I was going to be given an on-camera audition that would test my knowledge of current events. This time I went in prepared—overprepared, in fact. I spent so long providing commentary on my first question that the producer actually cut me off, saying, "That's enough for that topic; you're obviously very knowledgeable." I got the job. More importantly, I'd learned the lesson Dad had taught me. —JOSHUA SUNDQUIST

*Lord, when I'm facing an important decision, guide me through
the counsel of those who are wiser than I am.*

Do you need guidance for something specific? Seek the counsel of those who are wiser.

BEING AVAILABLE

So the Lord said to him, "What is that in your hand?" —EXODUS 4:2 (NKJV)

THE MOST POPULAR TECHNOLOGY IN MY CLASSROOM IS AN OLD-FASHIONED, hand-cranked pencil sharpener. I have to empty the shavings almost every day.

Who could have predicted that a stick of cedar seven inches long would be so useful for so many years to so many people: writers and editors, teachers and test takers, artists and composers, carpenters and puzzle masters?

Perhaps the greatest virtue of the pencil is its abundance. I'm never more than ten feet from a pencil. Almost three billion of them are manufactured every year in America alone.

The pencil is a good metaphor for one of the most treasured of character traits: availability. If I want to be a more valuable and useful person, I need to be more available.

"Will you teach my Sunday school class while I'm on vacation?"

"Yes, I can do that."

"Can I talk to you for a few minutes? It's important."

"Sure, have a seat."

"Could you give me a hand with these groceries?"

"You bet."

I don't need a college degree, movie-star looks, or money in the bank to be more useful. I just need to be handy.

When I say *yes*, I become a pencil in the hand of God and He can write His story through me. —DANIEL SCHANTZ

> *Yes, God, whatever You want me to do today, the answer is yes.*

For certain, the best ability is availability. Ask God to make you a pencil in His hand. Then rejoice in the story the two of you write together.

THE PLANS YOU HAVE FOR ME

By faith we understand that the universe was formed at God's command, so that what is seen was not made out of what was visible. —HEBREWS 11:3 (NIV)

A FEW DAYS AGO THERE WAS A MASSIVE JACKPOT THAT HAD FOLKS GOING crazy buying tickets. My friend Jaseem, whose father owns our little neighborhood newsstand and who is studying psychology in college, tells me, "Buying a ticket is hope-affirming. It makes people think that they could wake up in the morning to find their lives completely changed."

Except aren't we already supposed to be doing what we really want with our lives? I have nothing at all against people playing lotto. I caught my mother at it once, which, if you knew my mother, would have surprised you too. When I teasingly confronted her, she said that if she won the jackpot she would give it all to her church for programs to help the poor. That was Mom.

For me, at least, hope is the product of faith. I pray that I wake up every morning thinking that my life could be changed, not by a random number or a lucky hunch but by the grace of God. —EDWARD GRINNAN

Father, with You nothing is a gamble; nothing happens to us by chance.
Faith is the surest bet I know. Please help me live fully
the life You have planned for me.

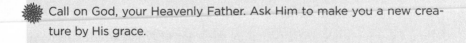 Call on God, your Heavenly Father. Ask Him to make you a new creature by His grace.

GOD'S CONSTANT LOVE

"Now choose life, so that you and your children may live and that you may love the Lord your God, listen to his voice, and hold fast to him. For the Lord is your life...." —DEUTERONOMY 30:19–20 (NIV)

WHEN I FIRST HEARD THE VOICE OF GOD, I WAS STUNNED, AS IF STRUCK BY lightning. I'd been participating in a small group discussion on having a personal relationship with God. His words were whispered deep within my soul and they changed my life: *Hal, I love you. Won't you love Me?*

Until then, I wasn't even sure God was real. But that encounter removed all my doubts, and I determined to learn all I could about this God Who loved me. So I began devouring the one source I felt would tell me everything I needed to know: the Bible.

Since that day thirty-nine years ago, God has spoken to me often, sometimes in quiet whispers, but mostly through Scripture. For instance, a passage in Deuteronomy suddenly sprang to life, leading me to leave my job as a newspaper reporter in Hawaii and move to California, not knowing what lay ahead. After I obeyed, I became a Bible smuggler for Brother Andrew. Later I joined *Guideposts* magazine, as God continued to guide.

My experience isn't unique. From books I've read and friends who've shared their journeys with me, I've learned that God desires a personal relationship with each of us. And so, I continue to seek Him in prayer and in His Word and listen for what He wants to tell me. —HAROLD HOSTETLER

Father, thank You for the Voice that assures me
of Your constant love.

 Read Deuteronomy 30:19–20 in several Bible translations. Then listen as God's voice speaks to *your* heart.

LEAD ON, LORD

My spirit abides among you; do not fear. —HAGGAI 2:5 (NRSV)

"I DON'T LIKE MY BIG-BOY BED." BENJI LAY STILL UNDER THE COVERS AND stared up at me.

The day before, I'd taken down his crib and rebuilt the toddler bed, which had sat disassembled in the closet ever since we'd bought a twin bed for Frances. At two, it was Benji's turn to leave behind a major prop of babyhood.

"I'm scared," Benji whispered. He missed the security of the crib. I missed the crib too. One of my favorite bedtime rituals was holding Benji during good-night prayers. Now we said prayers with him in bed.

Why was I in such a rush anyway? Yes, caring for a baby can be exhausting, and the glimpses we'd had of life with two kids instead of babies—hiking trips, playground games, days ungoverned by nap schedules—were tantalizing. But every milestone of life is like a little death. The past is unrecoverable. Why not try to slow things down?

"Want me to pick you up to say prayers?" I asked. Benji nodded. I picked him up and held him like always. His head burrowed into my neck. We said our thanks, our blessings. I laid him down and pulled up the covers. "Good night, little guy. I love you."

I paused at the door. Some things were different; some things were the same. All we could do was trust God to guide us through the changes.
—JIM HINCH

The world changes, but You remain ever faithful, Lord.

> Great is Thy faithfulness, Lord. Lead me as I enter the next chapter of my life.

TRUSTING GOD'S PLAN

He gives food to every creature. His love endures forever. —PSALM 136:25 (NIV)

IT WAS AN IMPOSSIBLE CHOICE: ADOPT A RESCUE DOG OR PICK OUT A PUPPY? At first, the answer had been clear. Brian and I had a fenced-in backyard and could give a home to a dog in need. We monitored the rescue Web sites.

Finally, tired of waiting for direction or guidance, we headed to north Georgia, where one litter of puppies was ready to leave their mom. As we looked for the rural address, we got a call—a miracle, really—in an area with little cell reception. It was the adoption agency telling us they had an eighteen-month-old golden retriever named Colby who was healthy, homeless, and ready to be loved. I told her we'd think about it.

Brian and I spent the next hour surrounded by furry bundles of energy whose teeth were so small we couldn't even feel them gnawing on our shoes. We held them, then looked at each other. These pups weren't for us.

We hopped in the car and headed for Atlanta, where we found Colby waiting for us. When we walked in the room, he came over and sat down between us, as if he'd known he was ours all along.

As I often do, I tried to rush God's plan, forcing a litter of puppies to fit into the hole in our family made just right for Colby.

As we packed Colby into the car and headed home, he crawled into my lap and I knew that this decision—God's decision—had been right all along.

—ASHLEY KAPPEL

Lord, thank You for the love animals bring into our lives.
We are blessed!

Make a vow to trust God's impeccable timing in an area of struggle within your life. Rehearse the promise so you can remember it.

GIVE THANKS

Rejoice always, pray continually, give thanks in all circumstances; for this is God's will for you in Christ Jesus. —1 THESSALONIANS 5:16–18 (NIV)

As I took off my sweater for the fourth time that morning, I tried to give thanks. "Thank You, God, for hot flashes." Oh, He could tell my heart was not in it. I tried again. "Thank You for the changes in my body." *Hmm. Yes. Thank You for these changes.*

I am changing, and it's rather fascinating. The last time I experienced this much physical change I was pregnant; before that it was adolescence. "Hey, God, how cool is being human? We grow over a lifetime. You created an amazing machine!"

Another hot flash surged through me. My face flushed and my back heated up. I pulled off my sweater again. Rather than getting upset, I was intrigued by the wonder of my body. I timed the heat wave—ninety seconds. It was not nearly as long as I had thought. My annoyance faded just a little.

Being thankful in all circumstances does not mean you have to like it. Being thankful means acknowledging the situation and doing your best to give thanks. With that prayer comes a response from God, an offering of peace.

I still have hot flashes and get annoyed with the drastic changes in my temperature, but when I remember to give thanks, it is easier. —LISA BOGART

*Dear Father God, saying thank You is a hard discipline. Remind me
that all of the circumstances in my life come from You and
that I can rejoice over them. Amen.*

Think about your physical transition and give thanks for a specific change that has come as a result of growing older.

DANCE AMID THE DISSONANCE

"Give us this day our daily bread." —MATTHEW 6:11 (NAS)

NINETEEN NEW GRADUATES FROM MERCER UNIVERSITY FLEW TO NORTHERN Thailand and will teach conversational English there. One of the most lush and beautiful environs, Thailand is also blessed with lovely and gracious people. Yet, for these young Americans, their new home is on the other side of the world and, for the first time, they are far away from family and security. Exotic novelty is now wearing off, and some write to me of loneliness and fear and second thoughts about leaving home. The reality of a brave new venture is seeping in.

So it is in life. A new job moves us to another state. A wonderful wedding flings us into adulthood, and we realize: *We can't go home again.* The retirement we have longed for casts us into uncharted waters, and we fear the future.

A friend once told me that when life quits changing and fear is conquered, there is a good chance you are dead. I think she is right. A rich life is always seasoned by the spices of apprehension, anxiety, and adjustment. Such painful emotions sing a rich duet with peace, security, and intimacy. Life is filled with paradox, and we must learn to dance amid the dissonance. —SCOTT WALKER

Father, give me the courage to weather those times
of apprehension with confidence. Amen.

 Try to imagine Jesus once and for all conquering the very issue that's been challenging you.

IN HIS TIME

Let the morning bring me word of your unfailing love, for I have put my trust in you. Show me the way I should go, for to you I entrust my life. —Psalm 143:8 (NIV)

THE PLAN WAS SIMPLE. I'D GO TO BIRMINGHAM, ALABAMA, FOR A THREE-DAY weekend to look at a dozen or so houses. Then my husband and I would go back a few weeks later to see the ones that passed the first round. Maybe, afterward, we'd put in an offer.

Instead, after thirty-six hours of looking, I'd found a house, put in an offer, and gone under contract, all without Brian having seen it.

"It's perfect!" I told him, and it was. It had everything on our lists, which we'd created as we diligently did our homework.

Brian packed a bag and told his boss, "I sent Ashley to look at houses, and it seems she's purchased one."

The boss replied, "Well, Brian, sounds like you'd better go see it!"

"Didn't you guys just test-drive cars for a year before buying?" his co-workers asked.

"I did," Brian replied as he rushed out, "but this time I sent Ashley!"

There are times when I try to make life more complicated. If I do all these steps, I think, then surely that is God's path. I'm ever thankful when God, Who knows my love of planning and order, thrusts me out of my comfort zone with a situation only He could align and whispers, *Go forward. Keep walking. Trust Me.* —ASHLEY KAPPEL

God, thank You for reminding me that Your time is the only time that matters.

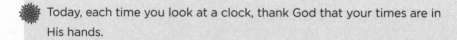 Today, each time you look at a clock, thank God that your times are in His hands.

LISTENING IN THE EVERYDAYNESS

And after the fire came a gentle whisper. —1 KINGS 19:12 (NIV)

WHAT MADE CORRIE TEN BOOM RISK HER LIFE TO SAVE JEWISH PEOPLE living in occupied Holland? *It must have been some great event,* I thought, *some dramatic soul-stirring call from God.*

"No," she said, "it was a simple, very ordinary moment."

By 1942, it was dangerous for Jews to appear in the streets of Haarlem. So Corrie, a watchmaker and repairer, started going to the homes of her Jewish customers to pick up and deliver work. One evening this took her to the house of a doctor and his wife. They were chatting over cups of rationed tea stretched with rose leaves, when from upstairs a child's voice piped, "Daddy, you didn't tuck us in!"

Excusing himself, the doctor hurried upstairs. Corrie and her hostess kept chatting. Nothing had changed. Everything had changed. At any minute, Corrie realized, there could be a knock at the door of *this* house. *This* mother, *this* father, *these* children could be herded into the back of a truck.

Still carrying on their conversation, still sipping tea, Corrie silently dedicated her life to the Jewish inhabitants of Holland. "Lord Jesus, I offer myself for Your people in any way, any place, any time."

Out of a daily domestic moment grew a heroine of the Dutch resistance, whose story of loss, suffering, and unstoppable joy inspires even today.
—ELIZABETH SHERRILL

> *God of joyful surprises, help me listen for Your voice in*
> *the everydayness of my life.*

Has God surprised *you* with joy lately? Release a balloon into the heavens in praise.

RECOGNIZING HIS BLESSINGS

Light in a messenger's eyes brings joy to the heart, and good news gives health to the bones. —PROVERBS 15:30 (NIV)

EVERY YEAR MY MOM SENDS OUT CHRISTMAS CARDS FEATURING FUN FAMILY updates, always with a positive spin. She highlights items such as Best Trip, Best Student, and Best Athlete, but the much-desired top spot is Best News, and every year the family has a good-natured battle over who will get recognized in that category.

For the last few years I've been in the running with key life-changing moves, like graduating from college or getting my first real job, but just as I started experiencing big changes, so did my siblings. Grandchildren started pouring in, and what's better news than a new baby in the family?

My mom has considered using vertical columns for everyone or doing away with the categories altogether, but she's been overruled time and again. This year I thought I might get the top spot for sure, thanks to my engagement, but then two new grandbabies swooped in. They're competing for the title and don't even know it!

As I sat wondering how I would do in next year's competition, having tossed my wedding into the hat, I realized how blessed our family is. How wonderful that we have so many good things happening that there are so many choices for the Best News spot! —ASHLEY JOHNSON

> *God, thank You for all of the blessings in my life and*
> *the vision with which to recognize them.*

List five things God has blessed you with this month. Thank Him for each one.

WISDOM TO DEAL WITH CHANGE

The Sovereign Lord is my strength; he makes my feet like the feet of a deer, he enables me to tread on the heights.... —HABAKKUK 3:19 (NIV)

FOR TWENTY-SEVEN YEARS, I HAD THE PRIVILEGE OF SERVING AS PRESIDENT of Mendenhall Ministries, a rural Christian community organization. For the past eleven years, I served as executive director and then president of Mission Mississippi. When I stepped down as president, the Mission Mississippi board allowed me to remain in a part-time position.

It was quite a change to move from being *the* decision maker to being just one of the people in the room. It sounds great to be able to serve without all the responsibility, but in practice it isn't easy to adjust. I'm asking God to give me wisdom to deal with these changes.

Habakkuk 3:19 has become a particularly important Scripture for me in this season of my life. I'm learning how to trust this sovereign Lord as I go on this journey. And my God is giving me the strength to walk without the titles, the position, or the authority, and to live out the meaning of being a servant, not just in theory, but in practical reality. —DOLPHUS WEARY

Lord, help me to continue to learn how to depend on You, and help me to offer everything to You, including my pride.

 Serve someone in your path today who didn't even ask for your help.

COURAGE TO LIVE YOUR BEST LIFE

For the Lord is our judge, the Lord is our lawgiver, the Lord is our king....
—ISAIAH 33:22 (NIV)

WHEN JACK AND I GOT MARRIED IN 2012, I WAS SIXTY-SIX YEARS OLD AND he was seventy-five. I didn't change my name, and we decided to keep both of our condos, which are just fifty-seven steps from each other. *What will my family and friends think of our living arrangement?* I worried.

We sleep and eat breakfast at Jack's condo but almost always have dinner at mine (I like my kitchen stuff better than his). I work in my office in my condo while he works on volunteer projects in his. We put our guests in the bedroom in my place. After dinner, Jack sometimes watches sports on TV at his condo while I watch something else in mine. We're back and forth every day, all day.

While browsing through the New Testament, I began to wonder how Jesus felt walking the land, gathering hundreds of people at a time, trying to talk them into living their lives in a completely different way...His way. Jesus was a renegade marching to the sound of a different philosophy.

Thinking of how Jesus lived His life gave me courage to live my life in a different way from that of my neighbors, friends, and family. I needn't have worried. Now that Jack and I have been living in both condos for a few years, many of our married friends wish they had two places to live in too!
—PATRICIA LORENZ

Father, thank You for the courage to live my life the way it works best for me and for the blessing of having two homes and one loving husband.

Make a courageous change in your own life based on God's will, not people's expectations.

LEADING ME THROUGH

The Lord your God is going ahead of you.... —DEUTERONOMY 1:30 (NLT)

WHEN I SAT DOWN TO WRITE MY RESOLUTIONS FOR THE NEW YEAR, I looked back through my journal to resolutions I'd made over the last twenty years. "*Hmm,*" I said to my friend who'd met with me so that we could write our resolutions together, "it seems that each year my resolutions are basically the same. Eat better, exercise more, and read my Bible daily." I shut my journal. "I don't want to write a laundry list of things to do this year."

"I have an idea," my friend said. "How about we write our resolutions based not on things to *do* but based on how to *be*?" She opened her journal. "A friend shared some ideas with me the other day. I think they are just what we are looking for." She read, "Be prayerful. Be trustful. Be obedient. Be forgiving. Be faithful. And, finally, be a follower of Jesus."

"Wow, these are great resolutions!" I said. "I must admit, though, they seem like a pretty tall order. I mean, without even knowing what will happen, we are resolving to handle everything this year as true followers of Christ. I love the idea, but it's a bit daunting."

"Let's remember this thought then," she said. "What's important about this new year is not *what* is ahead of us but *Who* is ahead of us."

With that, I became thankful for the guidance and began to embrace the coming year. —MELODY BONNETTE SWANG

Jesus, I know You will never lead me into anything
You won't lead me through. Help me to be a prayerful, trustful,
obedient, forgiving, faithful follower of You this year. Amen.

 Choose a word to guide you today based on *being*, not *doing*.

GIVE A BIT OF YOURSELF

And, fathers, do not provoke your children to anger, but bring them up in the discipline and instruction of the Lord. —EPHESIANS 6:4 (NRSV)

TWO YEARS AGO I WAS OFFERED A NEW JOB. IT PROMISED TO BE CHALLENGING and fulfilling and, yes, even fun—a tremendous opportunity and a blessing in every way. Well, every way but one: It was 142 miles from home, each way; 142 miles from my wife's ministry, 142 miles from my daughter's high school. Moving wasn't a viable option.

For weeks I wrestled with one key question: not salary or prestige or career tracks, but about being a dad. Was I being selfish to take the job? Didn't being a father take priority? How could I be a good father if I wasn't even home?

Twice I had the phone in my hand, ready to turn down the job, but hung up. Then one day I happened to find myself in the same room as someone I knew who was a terrific father. I wound my way over to him and when he turned and said hello, I told him about my situation. "What should I do?" I asked him.

He looked me straight in the eye and said, "You—and your daughter— don't need my advice. You need each other. If you can give each other that, as often as you can, with as much commitment as you can muster, you'll be fine."

I took the job. It's meant being away from home two, three, sometimes even four nights a week. That's been really hard on all of us. But here's what I've learned about being a father from being away: While kids think they need a lot of stuff, what they need most is you! And there are a million different ways to give a bit of yourself every day, whether you're home or not. —JEFF JAPINGA

Father God, as You have given freely to me, inspire me
to give of myself to my own children.

 Find a unique way to give of yourself today.

GOD PLANS AHEAD

Mercy and truth are met together; righteousness and peace have kissed each other.
—PSALM 85:10 (KJV)

WHEN MY HUSBAND, DAVID, MADE THE HEART-WRENCHING DECISION TO leave his post as senior minister at Hillsboro Presbyterian Church, the church was strong, thriving, and ripe for new leadership. But leaving was complicated.

No one has ever loved a congregation more than David, and the congregation responded in kind. So it was infinitely sad when an influential person began erasing David's legacy. We had looked forward to returning to Hillsboro after the proper transition period, but now the outlook was cloudy. Would it work for David to come back? Would we lose our church family forever?

Finally, a new minister was chosen. I wasn't sure how I would feel until I met Chris. My reaction was immediate. I have a pastor! *But what about David?*

Well, it seems God had planned ahead. Chris sent out a letter to the congregation, addressing the misperception that "it's not possible to love the new pastor if you still love the previous pastor." He dispelled that notion with five simple words: "It's okay to love both." Chris went on to describe his meetings with David and to announce that he had invited him to come back to Hillsboro, where the two of them "share a love for the church and its people."

And so it was finished. We had a church home once again, where we could come and worship with our family and friends, a place where there's enough love for everyone, and a new minister wise enough to know that's true. —PAM KIDD

Father, I pray for the day when all of us grasp the unlimited reservoir of Your love and can finally see its regenerating power.

Is there a situation in your life that has you feeling conflicted? Seek godly counsel.

PRACTICE LISTENING

To answer before listening—that is folly and shame. —PROVERBS 18:13 (NIV)

JULEE AND I HAD HAD A FIGHT. WE HADN'T EXACTLY HUNG UP ON EACH other, but almost. We were each pretty itchy to end the conversation first.

We don't like being mad at each other, and we don't fight like we used to when our marriage was new. But some days I wasn't sure our marriage would survive. But a wise mentor to whom I brought my problem offered me guidance.

"She's too emotional," I told him. "She takes everything personally."

After a few minutes, he said, "And what about you? A fight takes two. All you've talked about is Julee."

Well, I thought, *isn't she the problem?*

"I just defend myself," I said.

I wanted to take those words back immediately. My friend smiled. "That's why most couples fight," he said. "They're busy defending themselves and not listening. Try repeating back what you thought she said. See if you both hear the same thing. You won't stop fighting until you start understanding each other."

Listen rather than react. Understand instead of defend. Lo and behold, we stopped fighting and started talking things out more. We had our blowups for sure; now we knew how to call a truce. We had to *practice* not fighting.

Maybe I'm out of practice, I thought, picking up the phone to call Julee. It would be good to hear her voice. —EDWARD GRINNAN

God, You brought Julee and me together for a reason, and it wasn't to fight.
Help us keep our ears open so that our hearts may stay open too.

When you converse with someone today, tune out distractions and tune in to her or him.

GAINING INSIGHT

"Please test your servants for ten days: Give us nothing but vegetables to eat and water to drink." —DANIEL 1:12 (NIV)

LAST NIGHT I DREAMED OF COOKIES—NOT THE STORE-BOUGHT KIND OR even the bakery kind. These were the kind my son-in-law Paul bakes and sells: large oatmeal cookies with raisins, walnuts, and white chocolate-chip chunks.

So why am I dreaming of his cookies? I guess because I'd love one right now. But I won't have one; I'm dieting. When I stepped on the scale a few months ago and saw the numbers had edged up a bit, I knew it was time.

Sticking to my diet has taken a lot of discipline. I live close to New Orleans, a city known for its cuisine. As much as I wanted the French Market beignets with powdered sugar for breakfast, I ate a bagel instead. Turning down the Mardi Gras king cake was difficult. At lunch, I ate salads instead of the fried shrimp po'boys that everyone else ordered. *This is no fun,* I thought.

But then something changed: The discipline I practiced with my eating habits began to show up in other areas too. I started getting up early to read my Bible and pray before work; I walked through my neighborhood in the evenings; I even caught up with my correspondence.

I know now that the added weight reflected an undisciplined lifestyle. I needed to make better choices with food, exercise, and my free time. It hasn't been easy, but I'm grateful for the experience. I've lost a few extra pounds and gained a whole lot of insight. —MELODY BONNETTE SWANG

Lord, may I be mindful that when I say no to
an unhealthy lifestyle, I'm saying yes to You.

Make one small change today, and continue your effort for thirty days. That's officially how long it takes to form a new habit.

IN THE FATHER'S HANDS

For now we see through a glass, darkly; but then face to face: now I know in part; but then shall I know even as also I am known. —1 CORINTHIANS 13:12 (KJV)

THERE ARE DAYS WHEN I JUST DON'T KNOW WHO MY OLDEST DAUGHTER IS. When Elizabeth was singing in a children's choir, I'd ride home with her on the subway and get some hint of how her day had been. Lately, though, most of my questions get terse, generic answers: "Fine" or "Okay" or "Not bad."

A couple of weeks ago, we learned that Elizabeth, who is sixteen, had been admitted to college as an early decision/early admission applicant. So next year she'll be going off to another city to start school—and life—on her own.

I had just called home when the news arrived, and I heard Elizabeth's shout of joy. Suddenly I felt like Zero Mostel singing "Sunrise, Sunset." "Come on," I told myself, "you're just being sentimental." But that didn't stop the tears.

So next year I'll have to add a few hundred miles to the teenaged reticence between Elizabeth and me. Not that I'm worried. From what I can see and hear, Elizabeth's inner world is made up of math and physics, William Shakespeare, and the elaborate games based on *Star Wars* and *Star Trek* that she shares with her younger siblings. She loves music and movies and drawing her own comic books and singing silly songs. And as I sat next to her in church last Sunday and listened to her sing descants on "The First Noel," I knew that her faith had become as much a part of her as her sweet soprano voice. As for the rest, I can leave that—and Elizabeth—in her Father's hands. —ANDREW ATTAWAY

Lord, thank You for this wonder, this mystery You have given into our care.
Be with Elizabeth as she goes out on her own, now and always.

Is there a situation that has you perplexed at every turn? Imagine yourself placing it in God's big, capable hands.

ALL THINGS WORK FOR HIS GLORY

And we know that all things work together for good to those who love God, to those who are the called according to His purpose. —ROMANS 8:28 (NKJV)

"YOU WON'T BELIEVE IT." IT WAS LEMUEL, A GUIDEPOSTS OUTREACH STAFF member, calling me at home.

"Believe what?" I asked.

"This morning when I arrived at church, I was informed that this was the last Sunday service for the congregation." The interim pastor had resigned, and the congregation was unable to find another one. In addition, attendance and the church's financial stability had declined significantly. A decision was made that it was best to close the doors.

"How are the members?" I asked.

"Some are emotional, but most understand the practicality of this decision. How are you feeling?" Lemuel asked me. I'd left the church years ago as the pastor.

"I'm sad, disappointed, but to some extent I understand. My hope was that the church would continue its ministry for many years."

"Pablo, all things work for God's glory," Lemuel said to me. I struggled to accept the idea that closing our church would work together for God's glory. Yet I knew that God could turn difficult moments into opportunities for blessings.

"I think you are right," I said to Lemuel. "Although the church's ministry was brief, the impact of God's love on the people will live on." —PABLO DIAZ

Lord, You help us get through the unexpected and changing things. Thank You.

Write an encouraging note to someone for whom a door has abruptly closed.

BREATHE DEEPLY

My flesh and my heart fail; but God is the strength of my heart and my portion forever. —PSALM 73:26 (NKJV)

LIFE IS UP IN THE AIR THESE DAYS. WE HAVEN'T FOUND A THERAPEUTIC high school for John yet. Mary's ballet studio went through an acrimonious split, and she has to decide whom to side with. Andrew's still job-hunting. I'm not sure if we can afford to homeschool, and I just lost a freelance job. Yesterday, I spilled iced coffee on my laptop and damaged the keyboard.

I remind myself that things will work out somehow. We may have to move or make major adjustments to our lifestyle. But swallowing those changes is more likely to be foul-tasting than fatal. When I force myself to look my fears in the face, I know the real problem: I don't want to be as strong as God is asking me to be. I wish His provision included a middle-class comfort clause. It doesn't.

So I breathe deeply, pulling the air God made into the lungs He crafted. I inhale a prayer and exhale another, calling out to the Comforter, absorbing Him into my body and soul. *Come, Holy Spirit, fill the heart of Your servant and kindle in me the fire of Your love.* Whatever changes are looming, the change in my heart has to come first. —JULIA ATTAWAY

Come, Lord, and deepen my desire to live
in union with Your will.

 Introduce yourself to your greatest fear. Say something like, "Hello, fear. I'm a child of God and I can handle you."

MAKING THINGS RIGHT

"First go and be reconciled...." —MATTHEW 5:24 (NIV)

THE DOCTOR HAD GIVEN ME GOOD NEWS, BUT TO BE SAFE HE SUGGESTED A lab test. He sent me back to the waiting room to pick up a container, where I spoke to a receptionist I'd come to know almost as a friend. "I'll alert the lab," she said. We chatted briefly, and I took a seat and waited...and waited...and waited. The lab technician came out several times but called other patients. Meanwhile, the receptionist had gone on a break.

Finally, I went over to the relief receptionist. "How long does it take to pick up a specimen container? I've been waiting more than thirty-five minutes!"

She admitted that it shouldn't take so long. "I don't know what happened."

"Where can I file a complaint?" I demanded.

Just then the regular receptionist returned. Immediately, she apologized for misunderstanding my request, thinking I'd needed to speak with the technician. "I could have gotten the container myself," she said. "I'm so sorry."

Still fuming, I took the container and left. Afterward, though, I realized I was the one in the wrong. Ashamed, I prayed, *Lord, help me to make this right.*

Not an hour later the receptionist phoned to confirm an upcoming appointment for my wife. "I didn't know if I dared call," she said. I immediately asked her to forgive me for my actions and took the blame for not communicating clearly.

"Then we're still friends?" she asked, her voice brightening.

"You bet," I said. —HAROLD HOSTETLER

Father, whenever I'm in the wrong, help me to do the right thing.

 Have you complained and later learned you were in the wrong? It's still not too late to set the record straight.

LOVE ONE ANOTHER

Dear friends, let us love one another, for love comes from God. Everyone who loves has been born of God and knows God. —1 JOHN 4:7 (NIV)

I'VE ALWAYS BEEN SOMETHING OF A LONER. IN MIDDLE SCHOOL, I PREFERRED a good fantasy novel to time on the playground, and in college, I often chose to do homework or watch a movie rather than spend time with friends. Even at church, I chose to sit in pews toward the back, where I could pray alone. Sometimes my desire to be on my own was so strong that I would snap at people just to get them to leave me alone.

I'd like to say all that changed when I met Emily, that her warmth and beauty opened my heart so wide I couldn't hold it in any longer. But it didn't, at least not at first. It took weeks of hanging out together before I worked up the courage to ask her out, and even when we started dating, I still found myself drawing away.

After a night when I raised my voice at Emily for simply asking if we could have dinner together, I knew I had to change. Not only was I endangering the most important relationship in my life, but I wasn't living by Christ's precept to love and care for one another.

I didn't become a new person overnight. It took months of work and prayer to stop pushing Emily away. Ultimately, I had to accept that I wanted to watch her laugh as much as anything on earth—and I would change, in any way necessary, to protect and keep her in my life with God's help. My relationship with Emily—and my family and friends—is ongoing... —SAM ADRIANCE

Thank You, Lord, for always leaving Your heart open for me, thereby teaching me to open my heart to others.

 Open your heart wide today. Someone most dear is standing outside.

GRACE IN A CHANGING WORLD

"It is the Spirit who gives life; the flesh is no help at all. The words that I have spoken to you are spirit and life." —JOHN 6:63 (ESV)

ISAIAH, MY FIVE-YEAR-OLD SON, WAS LEARNING TO READ. THE WHOLE WORLD began to unfold for him. In the grocery store, he'd move through the aisle, his pointer finger gliding over the smooth surfaces of cereal boxes. In the van, he'd sound out the names of storefront signs. At home, he'd sit in our home-school classroom, sputtering digraphs and diphthongs and stringing sounds into words.

"Dogs. Big dogs. Little dogs. Big and little dogs," he read. He sat on a small wooden chair. His head dipped low and his blond bangs fell in his eyes. When he finished a sentence, he punctuated the ending with a lift of the head and a brighter-than-the-sun smile.

Words. They were changing Isaiah's life. They opened new doors of learning, of self-sufficiency, of pleasure and freedom and bliss. I curled on the sofa beside his chair, nearly as excited as he.

Isaiah finished the page and closed the book. Then he erupted from his chair. His arms wrapped around my neck, and his breath was sweet and warm on my ear. "I'm doing it, Mama!" he said. "See how I've grown?"

I held him tight. Growing and changing by the power of words—that's a precious thing. —SHAWNELLE ELIASEN

Lord, thank You for Your life-changing Word. Amen.

Reread a favorite children's book. Why not one that has a wonderful adult message like *The Giving Tree* or *The Velveteen Rabbit*?

WHEN GOD SENDS A MESSAGE

My dear brothers and sisters, be strong and immovable. Always work enthusiastically for the Lord, for you know that nothing you do for the Lord is ever useless. —1 CORINTHIANS 15:58 (NLT)

I'VE LONG BELIEVED THAT GOD SENDS PEOPLE INTO OUR LIVES. SOMETIMES I don't recognize them as quickly as I should; at other times it's obvious. This past year I had the privilege of meeting Kent Annan, a missionary to Haiti.

I first heard about Kent from a friend, an avowed agnostic who'd read Kent's book *Following Jesus through the Eye of the Needle* and knew I'd enjoy the story. I ordered the book and started to read it in fits and starts.

Then a month later someone else mentioned Kent's name and mailed me a copy of the book. I'd gotten the message: God wanted me to read the book. I did and was touched by the powerful message. Then I discovered that Kent Annan lived nearby. I got in touch with him, and we met for lunch.

As we shared the meal, Kent told me that his father was a pastor. Kent had lived a pretty normal life before his call to the mission field. He'd never rebelled against his family or his God. His spiritual life, Kent said, had been filled with "little conversions" that drew him closer to God and lit his own life path.

I thought about what Kent shared that day and realized I've had little conversions too. They were the quiet mornings when I prayed and felt His presence and His love, guiding me, urging me to step forward in faith, and assuring me He would always be at my side. —DEBBIE MACOMBER

Thank You, Father, for Your presence and peace, and for the confidence that comes with knowing that You are always with me.

 Have you experienced little conversions in your life? Share your journey.

KNOW THE "I AM" GOD

Be still, and know that I am God.... —PSALM 46:10 (KJV)

I SPOKE TO A FRIEND ABOUT MY STRUGGLES TO PRAY, AND SHE SHARED WITH me an experience she had when her mother was in the hospital, fighting cancer. Molly told me that every day she would go to the chapel in the hospital. When she got there, however, she found herself too afraid to pray. She couldn't find the words. She didn't even want to say, "Thy will be done."

"What if God's will was to take my mother?" she said to me. "I couldn't pray for that." Molly would sit there, with her hands folded tightly in front of her face and her eyes pressed shut, afraid to have a complete thought pass through her mind.

Then one day, she noticed an inscription in the chapel: "Be still, and know that I am God."

"This," Molly said, "was something I could pray. I would just repeat those words over and over."

Hearing my friend's story gave me fresh meaning for that Scripture and a new outlook on praying. I was trying to force a connection with God through a series of words.

My pastor says, "Prayer is the soul's sincere desire to commune with God." Since my soul desires, I only need to be still and allow the opportunity.

—NATALIE PERKINS

*Lord, thank You for continuing to provide me with guidance
that draws me nearer to You.*

Find a quiet place to pray for guidance and then listen for God's direction.

GUIDANCE FROM BEYOND THE STARS

Remember now thy Creator in the days of thy youth.... —Ecclesiastes 12:1 (KJV)

"Well, what about *your* undergraduate career?"

It's a question my college students ask, and I have yet to give them an honest answer—well, an *unvarnished* answer. I can tell them quite honestly that it was a long time ago (accurate) and I don't remember (also accurate), but I'm not about to tell them why.

It's odd: I turned eighteen, and suddenly it was deemed that I could vote, go off to war, drive past midnight, stay out all hours. But I wasn't ready for any of that. I doubt many of us are. Instead, I pinballed from one mistake to another, bouncing indelicately through late adolescence with all its attendant charms and dangers. I would love, love, love to steer my students clear of the subterranean rocks and riptides that threaten their journey; I cannot. They'll have to find them for themselves.

And now my oldest daughter is in college and my middle daughter is ready to join her. Well, *not* ready, but as ready as she'll ever be. My experienced, postcollegiate heart often finds itself in my throat as I watch my kids venture out together: me waving from the shore, trying to warn them of the terrible currents that they must navigate themselves, and whispering prayers like every traveler and every parent who seeks guidance from something beyond the stars. —Mark Collins

Lord, help me not to be the only one who learns from my mistakes.

If your children or any young person comes to you for advice, guide them in God's direction.

Father, I need Your guidance today. I have sought the counsel of Your Word in the Bible. And yet I do not want to go forward until I have brought my decision before You in prayer. I seek Your peace upon my heart and mind that I am doing the right thing. If this is not the right thing for me, I pray that You make me restless and unsure until I have prayed it through and found Your peace. Help me not to lean on my own understanding, but to wait until You direct my path (Proverbs 3:5–6). Amen.

KAREN BARBER

Chapter 9

WHEN YOU FEEL ANGRY

....

Anger devours almost all other good emotions. It deadens the soul. It numbs the heart to joy and gratitude and hope and tenderness and compassion and kindness.

JOHN PIPER

SALT AND LIGHT

If I speak in the tongues of men or of angels, but do not have love, I am only a
resounding gong or a clanging cymbal. —1 CORINTHIANS 13:1 (NIV)

I WAS MAD. SEETHING, REALLY. MY FRIEND HAD POSTED A COMMENT ON
Facebook that really stung. I was ready to put on my boxing gloves.

I typed a sarcastic response and quickly hit Post. There! At least I had stuck
up for what was right.

Five minutes later, I got a phone call. It was my friend in tears, explaining
to me that she had never intended her original comment to come across the
way it had. She had been in the middle of dealing with sick kids and a pushy
boss and had typed words that she never meant to say. And I had responded
like a sixth grader on the playground. Oh, the power of social media!

Making amends with my friend was the easy part. But the angry words that
I had so publicly aired were harder to take back, clashing against the truthful
and loving words that I should've said in the first place—words that would've
promoted peace and love instead of discord. —ERIN MACPHERSON

Lord, please sprinkle my words with salt and light,
and eliminate hurtful or angry words from my vocabulary
so that I can speak Your truth and love to my friends.

What words do you find to be most encouraging? Work on replacing
angry responses with edifying responses that we all can use.

SEEING A BETTER WAY

"But I say to you, Love your enemies and pray for those who persecute you, so that you may be children of your Father in heaven...."—MATTHEW 5:44–45 (NRSV)

WHEN I NEED TO REMEMBER SOMETHING AND DON'T HAVE A NOTEPAD nearby, I take off my wedding ring and slip it in my pocket or put it on my desk where I can see it. It may sound ridiculous, but since the ring represents the second-most-important relationship in my life, I'm very aware of it. Like my marriage, the ring is a part of me, and I often touch or turn it around my finger during the day. So when it's off, I'm sure to remember why I took it off.

Recently I folded my hands in prayer and noticed that my ring *was* off. I reached into the pocket where I'd put it earlier that day and remembered why it was there. I'd been hurt by a colleague and I wanted to make sure I remembered every rotten detail so that I could tell my husband, Charlie, and we could discuss various ways to, well, get revenge. And all this came flooding back simply because I'd routinely folded my hands in prayer. Except that with God, nothing about prayer is routine.

I can't say that my anger and hurt evaporated right then and there, but when I finally did see Charlie later that evening, I had more than one interesting thing to remember to tell him. —MARCI ALBORGHETTI

Father, when I'm determined to go in a negative direction,
please turn me gently around so that I can see a better way.

 When someone angers you, take a deep breath, or many deep breaths, and ask God to gently turn you from your anger to see a better way.

CHANGE THE TONE OF THE DAY

A gentle answer turns away wrath, but a harsh word stirs up anger.
—PROVERBS 15:1 (NIV)

MY HUSBAND WOKE UP GRUMPY THIS MORNING, WHICH MADE ME GRUMPY. Lynn came into the kitchen earlier than usual, which interrupted my sacred time of solitude, surrounded by my Bible, journal—all my stuff.

"What are you doing up so early?" I asked.

"I don't feel well."

"You don't ever feel well when you first wake up," I reminded him.

"And I don't like these jeans. They don't fit right," he said.

"We spent a whole afternoon at the store, trying on jeans and getting just the right ones. That's how they're supposed to fit."

"Well, they don't fit. You might like them, but I don't."

I knew my patience was waning, so I gathered my stuff and stomped off to a place where I could be alone and get holy.

I could still hear Lynn, so I talked to God. *You can change the tone of this day*, I imagined God saying to me. "But it's not my fault. Why should I apologize for Lynn's grumpiness?" Nothing in me wanted to take the first step.

I went back in the kitchen to refill my coffee cup. Lynn looked at me with a sort of question mark on his face, which made me laugh. "I'm sorry you don't feel well," I said.

"Thanks for understanding," he replied. And the day got better from there.
—CAROL KUYKENDALL

Lord, thank You for helping us change the tone of the day to one of joy.

If you feel anger rising in you, find a way to let off steam! Go for a brisk walk, tell a friend what's bugging you, attack the weeds in your garden.

SIT ON YOUR ANGER

Fools give full vent to their rage, but the wise bring calm in the end.
—PROVERBS 29:11 (NIV)

IT WAS LATE AFTERNOON AT THE NASHVILLE ZOO, AND MY FIVE-YEAR-OLD grandson, Frank, had his favorite place all to himself. It has nothing to do with the animals: It's the wall-to-wall tumbling mats in the playground area. He'd just finished building an obstacle course with every one of the uniquely shaped pillows.

"Watch this action, Granny," he called to me, knees bent, arms spread.

But his takeoff was interrupted by a mother and her young daughter striding across the mats. To my shock, the mother snatched the biggest and best pillow right out of Frank's obstacle course. "Do you mind if my child plays with this?" she asked brusquely.

She can't treat my grandson like that, I thought, and in anger I rose from the bench ready to let her know it. But Frank beat me to it.

"Would you like to play with me?" he asked the dark-haired little girl peering around her mother.

The girl nodded, giving Frank a wide smile. Sheepishly the mother handed back the pillow. Quietly, I sat down. The pillow debacle had ended before it began. The children came together to put on a tumbling show for two chastened adults, who were reminded that playing together is what it's all about.

—SHARI SMYTH

Lord, when friction divides, help me to still my tongue and sit
on my anger long enough to see what's really important.

❋ Talk to the kid that still lives inside your heart about something that makes you angry. Trust your childlike faith to get an answer on how to deal with it.

OFFER COMFORT INSTEAD

"You have covered yourself with anger.... You have covered yourself with a cloud so that no prayer can get through."—LAMENTATIONS 3:43–44 (NIV)

ONE DAY I SPOTTED AN ACQUAINTANCE AND PRIVATELY PRIDED MYSELF ON remembering her name. "Hi, Ingrid," I said. "How nice to see you again."

Ingrid returned my smile with a scowl and a fierce retort: "Nobody asked me if I wanted to be included in any of the women's circles. Just take my name off the list!" Then, without another word, she stalked off.

My surprise turned into anger. *What was that all about?* Granted, we attended the same church, but I'd had nothing to do with assigning anyone to a specific circle group. *I greeted her nicely. She had no right to snap at me like that!*

I was still seething when, a week later, I learned that Ingrid's husband had left her. Her unexpected response had nothing to do with me; I merely happened to be there when her anguish erupted. I should have followed her and said, "Ingrid, let's have lunch, and you can tell me what's the matter."
—ISABEL WOLSELEY

Lord, help me to remember that when someone has an
uncharacteristic flash of anger, it often means
that person needs a kind word of comfort.

 Some people you may meet today will make it difficult to offer them a smile or a kind word. Offer it anyway.

PRAYING FOR ENEMIES

*"But to you who are listening I say: Love your enemies, do good to those who hate you, bless those who curse you, pray for those who mistreat you." —*LUKE 6:27–28 (NIV)

I'VE BEEN DEEPLY CONCERNED FOR MY FRIEND. HER TEENAGE DAUGHTER has moved in with her older boyfriend and his dad. The boyfriend and his dad treat my friend with hostility. To make matters worse, my friend's ex-husband has joined them in their anger at her. Together they've leveled false accusations against my friend and have alienated her daughter from her.

Over the past months my friend has poured out her despair to me. Tonight, however, when I phoned her, I heard an amazing change in her voice. "I feel as though a huge weight has been lifted off me," she said.

"What happened?" I asked incredulously.

"Well, when I heard the Gospel reading at church this morning—to love your enemies and to pray for those who persecute you—I knew that somehow I had to do what Jesus said, even though it seemed impossible."

"Considering how you've been treated, it does seem impossible to do."

"I felt that I couldn't but that God could. For the rest of the service, I prayed for them. When I came home, I still felt overwhelmed by my hurt and anger, so I prayed more. Instead of praying for them to change, I simply asked God to do good to them.

"Suddenly, everything inside me changed. I felt a lightness I've never felt before. I know that somehow everything will work out. I'll keep praying for them and trusting God. I finally have peace." —MARY BROWN

Thank You, Lord, for helping my friend—and me—to obey
Your Word, even when it seems impossible.

Write Matthew 5:44 down on a piece of paper and tuck it into your pocket. Refer to it often.

FREE TO LOVE, FREE TO FOLLOW

My house shall be called... the house of prayer. —MARK 11:17 (KJV)

As I ENCOUNTER MARY OF MAGDALA IN MY DREAM TONIGHT, SHE SEEMS troubled.

"I can hardly believe what I saw today at the temple just the day after my Jesus had ridden into the holy city, so humbly and yet so triumphantly!

"Standing outside, I saw Him angrily stride into the outer court of the temple, cast out the people buying and selling there, overturn the tables of the money changers and the seats of those selling doves. Then He spoke: 'Is it not written, My house shall be called the house of prayer? But you have made it a den of thieves.'

"Never before have I seen Him so angry!"

I share your surprise, Mary. Jesus's actions in the temple raise a question in me: *Is anger ever justified?* I remember once confessing my anger to a minister. His reply surprised me: "May God deliver you from the *sting* of your anger but not from the *protection* of it."

I have since come to know that there are times when anger serves. Now, when I feel anger within me, I ask God, "Does this anger serve in some unmistakable way? Or does it just sting the other person...and me?" I know this only helps when I take time to listen for His guidance. When I fail to listen and let my anger guide me instead, it stings both me and the one with whom I'm angry. —MARILYN MORGAN KING

> *When I feel anger rising in me, Father, may I remember to ask,*
> *"Does this anger serve or sting?" Then may I listen for*
> *Your wisdom and follow Your truth.*

Consider something that's angered you in the recent past and how much energy you've used focusing on it. Ask yourself whether it's been worth the time.

RETHINK YOUR ANGER

For it is by grace you have been saved, through faith—and this is not from yourselves, it is the gift of God. —EPHESIANS 2:8 (NIV)

IT SHOULD HAVE BEEN A TOUCHING GOOD-BYE. INSTEAD, I WAS ARGUING with my three-year-old over his refusal to give my parents a hug. It seemed ridiculous to try to force my son into a warm, affectionate embrace, but I did it anyway. "Give Grandma and Papa a hug right now or you're in big trouble!" His scowl didn't melt into sweetness, which only made my own scowl even worse. "Fine! Get in the car!" I scolded. "That is so mean!"

Hours later when we arrived home, I was still hurt. My parents had done nothing but shower my son with love, kindness, gifts, and tons of candy. There was no reason for him to be so cold. I called my mother to apologize again for his behavior.

"Oh, Karen, don't be upset," my mother said. "I know he loves me. He will always be my little baby."

I felt the weight come off me, knowing that her unconditional love for my son was even greater than mine at that point. It not only made me rethink my anger, but it brought to mind God's grace. Hadn't I sometimes withheld my affection and appreciation from Him like a grouchy child? Yet God's unconditional love always prevailed. —KAREN VALENTIN

Thank You, Lord, for giving us a place in Your heart,
not by our works, but by Your mercy and grace.

Forgive yourself for the last meltdown. Acknowledge it for what it was so you can move on.

DON'T LET ANGER REIGN

Be not quick in your spirit to become angry, for anger lodges in the heart of fools.
—ECCLESIASTES 7:9 (ESV)

ONE OF THE ROUGHEST PERIODS OF MY LIFE WAS THE YEAR I SPENT unemployed after college graduation. If I had to choose one emotion to best sum up that time, it wouldn't be frustration, sadness, or worry; it would be anger. I went to college with the expectation that not only would I achieve personal growth, but I would also be set for the rest of my life. Falling short of those goals fueled my bitterness.

"Keep applying. That's all you can really do," my family and friends told me.

The best advice came, as usual, from my mother. "God will give you an opportunity soon that will make all of this worth it," she said.

Eventually, I landed a job at a real-estate company. It wasn't my dream job, but it paid the bills, kept me sane, and, best of all, gave me the experience I needed to get the position I have now at my alma mater, New York University.

Once the anger had subsided, it was easier to view the experience from another perspective. I was able to see how much support I can rely on from my family and friends. And, most important, I achieved a level of personal growth after college that I hadn't attained during those four years as an undergrad.

Life isn't always smooth or fair. But I'm learning not to allow anger to reign when life's difficult, and to trust that God is preparing amazing opportunities for me. —ERIK CRUZ

Thank You, Lord, for loving me when I'm foolishly blind to the opportunities You lay at my feet. Be patient with me.

Are you frustrated with God? His timing? His plan for your life? Let Him know so He can give you the tools you need to be patient.

THE BEAUTY OF A CONTRITE HEART

In your anger do not sin. —EPHESIANS 4:26 (NIV)

I EXPLODED AT ONE OF MY KIDS THIS AFTERNOON. THE CHILD HAD BEEN difficult for two hours and had given me plenty of provocation, but I was beyond mad. Fortunately, one of my other children shouted, "Mom, you have to stop!" So I grabbed a jacket and left the apartment, trusting that if my heart could not move itself to a better place, my feet could do the job.

It was pouring, and I strode into the wind in fierce, long steps. The cold rain did not wash away my anger. Ten minutes into my adrenaline-driven power walk, an observation slipped into my thoughts: *The strength of my reaction was out of proportion to the offense given.* I pushed the idea away like the wet hair falling into my eyes, but it returned to drip uncomfortably in my mind.

A block later, I stopped under a store awning, smeared my glasses clean with a wet finger, and considered the facts. My child had done wrong, and I had legitimate reason to be upset. But a few drops of righteous anger had been lost in a torrent of self-righteous indignation. *Show me the difference, Lord. I can see my child's sin. Show me mine.*

I sighed and shivered. The part of my heart that moments before had burned with anger now stung with cold, sticky regret. *I'm sorry, Lord. I am so sorry.* I turned toward home and caught a glimpse of myself in a storefront window. I did not look beautiful, and, yet, I did. For a contrite heart is a glorious thing, and what the rain can't wash clean, Jesus can. —JULIA ATTAWAY

Lord, cleanse my heart of the seeds of sin.

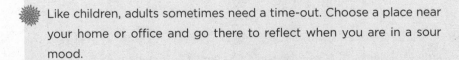
Like children, adults sometimes need a time-out. Choose a place near your home or office and go there to reflect when you are in a sour mood.

TEMPERING MY TEMPER

Be quick to listen, slow to speak, slow to anger. —JAMES 1:19 (NRSV)

OUR FAMILY HAS OWNED (OR BEEN OWNED BY) THREE SETS OF DOGS. WITH our first two dogs, I was quick to speak and quick to anger. I spoke to the second set a little more calmly and could often control my anger. We now have two dogs, Shadow and Coco, who are puppies in behavior but adult in size—a dangerous combination.

On the first nice day last spring, I rode my bike to our mailbox, about a mile down a gravel road from our house. On the way, Shadow ran into my front tire, turning it ninety degrees and sending me sailing over the handlebars. He sped home, barking frantically, and then stood by the door and continued to bark. Since none of our dogs had ever acted like Lassie before, my wife ignored him. When I hobbled home an hour later, Shadow slinked away and hid from us.

I returned from the hospital with a broken collarbone, a torn pectoral muscle, seven stitches in my elbow, and abrasions on my left leg from ankle to hip. Shadow slowly approached me, his head down and his tail between his hind legs, whimpering as he knelt beside me. I petted him with one hand and marveled at the new spirit God has created in me these past twenty years. It's a spirit that is sometimes—not yet always, but sometimes—quick to listen, slow to speak and slow to anger. —TIM WILLIAMS

Dear God, I thank You—and my pets thank You—
for tempering my temper.

Remember a time when you were able to thwart an angry response. Refer to that memory when you need it.

A CRY OUT TO HEAVEN

Out of my distress I called on the Lord; the Lord answered me and set me free.
—PSALM 118:5 (RSV)

THERE WERE NO WORDS FOR THE ANGER I FELT AS I STOOD IN DOWNTOWN Harare, watching children emerge from back alleys and storm drains. They came in waves, digging through trash bins, retrieving dirty bottles and cups. Soon the lady who brought tea and bread would be chugging up in her dilapidated car to fill the dirty bottles with morning tea.

God had beckoned me to Zimbabwe to write about the street children. But this was more than I could bear, and all my anger was focused in one direction—straight up to heaven.

I was armed with a writing pad, yet words couldn't describe the scene before me. My camera was strung over my shoulder, but film could never capture what I was seeing. Still, if I was going to make people understand what was going on in this AIDS-ravaged country, a photograph would be my most powerful tool.

My anger boiled as I grabbed my camera. "Okay, God, if You think I have something to give, You take the picture!" I held the camera and clicked.

Back home I spread the freshly developed prints across the kitchen table. There it was: an AIDS child was looking straight into my eyes.

In the years since, the face of that child has been in newspapers, on TV, in books and magazines. It's raised more money for kids in Africa than I can count. I'd like to take credit for the picture and be considered a great photographer, but I can't. It's God's photo, plain and simple. —PAM KIDD

Father, I called out in distress. You answered. What more can I say?

What injustice makes you mad? Find a like-minded organization and find a way to support it.

THE PEACE ONLY HE CAN GIVE

"I have told you these things, so that in me you may have peace. In this world you will have trouble. But take heart! I have overcome the world."
—JOHN 16:33 (NIV)

A WAVE OF TERROR RUSHED THROUGH MY BODY WHEN I HEARD MY MOTHER say that word.

"Cancer?" I repeated into the phone. "Papi has cancer?"

Mom did her best to assure me that the doctors had caught it early enough, but that didn't stop my tears. All I wanted to do was get on a plane to Florida and run into my father's arms.

"Karen," my mother said, with an uncharacteristic calm in her voice, "he's going to be fine." The absolute peace and assurance in her voice did more than calm me down; it puzzled me.

When I was growing up, my mother had thought every bump, cough, or pain was cancer. "Oh no, no," she'd say, frantic with worry as she'd examine us. "That doesn't look right. You need to get that checked!" She'd completely freak out over a small rash on my arm or a stomach bug, but now my father had cancer and she was calm?

For a moment it angered me. With all the years of her overreacting over nothing, she finally had a real reason to panic. Yet there was no hint of worry in her voice. The anger left just as quickly as I realized how unnatural this was for her. Only God could create such a shift in her response. —KAREN VALENTIN

Thank You, Lord, for the peace only You can give.

※ Meditate on Romans 15:13. Allow the peace and hope found in that verse to fill your mind.

LORD, NUDGE ME

"But if you forget about yourself and look to me, you'll find both yourself and me."
—MATTHEW 10:39 (MSG)

I GRIPPED THE STEERING WHEEL OF MY VEHICLE AS I FLEW DOWN THE highway. Mile after mile of gray wooden fence posts supporting strands of barbed wire flashed past. The road wound through large ranches with cattle grazing in the grassy meadows. The scenery looked peaceful, but I wasn't. I churned like a volcano ready to erupt. I'd been involved in a situation where I'd been repeatedly wronged and was driving to calm down.

I shook my head and raised my voice. "But, God, I…" I ranted about my situation and then I slapped the steering wheel and yelled, "I'm finished!"

Finally I grew quiet. Only the humming of the tires on the road broke the silence. *It's really not about what you want,* I heard. *It's about what I want to do through you. When you talk about I, I, I, each one of those I's is like those miles of fence posts. When you rant and rave, you're stringing barbed wire between us. You've been fencing Me out.*

Tears streamed down my face. "Oh, God, I'm so sorry. What do You want me to do?"

Stay and be a witness for Me.

I stayed. My situation didn't change. But I took control of my thoughts; I refused to go down the dark road of rage. Trusting the Lord and obeying Him despite my own desires brought me more joy than I could have imagined.
—REBECCA ONDOV

> *Lord, nudge me when I start putting I's*
> *where there should be Yous. Amen.*

❋ Hang a peaceful reminder around your rearview mirror to help you remain calm and focused while driving.

PLANTING LIGHT IN DARK HEARTS

I have no pleasure in the death of the wicked; but that the wicked turn from his way and live. —Ezekiel 33:11 (ESV)

I sit by the river for a long time, remembering my three friends turned to floating ash on this day ten years ago, murdered by a coward now hiding in a cave. People in the five boroughs of New York City breathed in the sinewy bodies of my friends, strapping hilarious Irish American boys, now dust. Their wives sleep alone, and their children have set one fewer plate at the table night after night, year after year. The scars on those children's hearts…

The rage starts to bubble up in me, and I sit down and watch the birds. "When furious, get curious," as my grandpa used to say. There are finches in the currant bushes, stuffing themselves. One finch gobbles so many currants it can hardly get aloft, and I start to laugh as it plummets slowly toward the river below. You never saw a fatter flailing finch in your life.

Against the whole welter of death and sadness, there are always finches in the bushes, mooing with happiness at the exquisite forest of fruit provided by the Master Orchardist. What could be a more eloquent prayer than that?

And while almost every atom in me wishes to wreak vengeance on the man who murdered my friends, a few brave atoms deep inside me believe that even he can awaken to the Light that made those finches and my friends; even he can emerge from the bloody arrogant shell in which he lives each day.

Life defeats death, hope defeats despair, light defeats darkness. There are always finches in the bushes. —Brian Doyle

> *Dear Lord, thank You for really fat finches. Thank You for reaching into dark hearts and planting light.*

 Sit outside and look, really look, at the natural world.

FEED YOUR SHEEP

Feed the flock of God which is among you, taking the oversight thereof.
—1 PETER 5:2 (KJV)

THE 101-DEGREE HEAT WASN'T NEARLY AS HOT AS THE RAGE THAT BOILED inside me. I reached into the stall and gently ran my fingers over the bony horse's hide. Three emaciated gray-and-brown horses crowded the stall. They could only be fed small amounts of low-energy food at a time because rich food would kill them.

Some of the herd died before the sheriff's department seized more than thirty others and brought them to the Hamilton, Montana, fairgrounds. Local veterinarians and we volunteers were nursing them back to health.

As I scratched the horse's forehead, an inquisitive man wearing a tan cowboy hat peered into the stall. "What kind of person would willingly starve them?"

I agreed and was going to say some unkind words when my spirit arrested me and a still, small voice said, *Look at the people around you. Many of them are starving to death spiritually. Will you have compassion and feed them?*

I looked at the folks crowding the fairgrounds. I'd never thought about people being spiritually emaciated. I could apply the same guidelines to their spiritual hunger as we did to the horses: If someone was spiritually starving, I could give him or her a teaspoon of God's love.

That afternoon a business contact mentioned that his son would soon go to Iraq. I wasn't familiar with his beliefs, but I asked if he would like me to pray for his son. It was a morsel of God's mighty Word. —REBECCA ONDOV

Teach me, Lord, how to make opportunities to feed Your sheep.

Fill a teaspoon with honey or another treat. As you enjoy its taste, envision it being a teaspoon of God's love.

SAVE ME FROM PRESUMPTION

If any one imagines that he knows something, he does not yet know as he ought to know. —1 CORINTHIANS 8:2 (RSV)

THE MORNING BEGAN WITH MY NOW DAILY TRIP TO THE ICU, WHERE MY quadriplegic sister tries to fight off pneumonia with a ventilator and her own iron will. (If the image of a woman who can move only her elbows seems beyond tragic, add a respirator and take away her speech. The lexicon has no words for this. I checked.)

Which is worse: helplessness or rage? The former hurts, but the latter sticks. In my family's case you'd think years of practice would give us an edge; we've had plenty of dress rehearsals for her death. If the average person spends two years of life waiting in lines, then my family has spent four decades waiting in drab-colored rooms with big windows and industrial carpet, waiting for visiting hours or blood tests or surgeons or answers or miracles. Mostly miracles.

And I've spent twice that amount of time in church waiting and praying.

On days like today, sitting bumper to bumper on the Parkway East on my way to work, prayer seems like an ill-timed joke. God reminds me of an absentee landlord who's put me in a windowless cold-water flat with no heat and no chance at subletting—except maybe to my sister, who'd welcome the change.

Somewhere near my exit, I remember *The Book of Common Prayer*: "Lord, save us from the presumption of coming to this table for solace only, and not for strength; for pardon only, and not for renewal." —MARK COLLINS

Lord, save me from the presumption of knowing what's best and worst.
Save me from the presumption of knowing.

Close your eyes and ask God to "take the wheel" when you are facing a challenge today.

GIVEN THE RIGHT WORDS

Thy brother's anger turn away from thee. —GENESIS 27:45 (KJV)

THE GUESTS AT THE MONASTERY WE VISIT ARE LIKE A FAMILY, SHARING living space and meals in the guesthouse. Over the period of a stay—whether for days or weeks—we get to know one another pretty well. Sometimes that can be a strain.

Before Christmas some years ago, my husband, Keith, and I uncomfortably shared the house with another couple and their ten-year-old daughter. The girl was a sweetheart, but her father criticized her all the time, sometimes even yelling at her.

When the Christmas tree was brought in, a priest supplied boxes of ornaments, and he, the daughter, and I began to decorate the tree. Her parents sat on the couch, watching us. The girl was relaxed, laughing, really enjoying herself. And then one of the glass ornaments slipped out of her hand and shattered on the floor. She froze, looking immediately at her father.

Before anyone else could say anything, I laughed and said, "Well, that's one! Last year, we broke three!"

The tension seemed to drain away. "I'll get the dustpan," the priest said. "Or do you think I should wait until we've broken more ornaments?"
—RHODA BLECKER

Thank You, Lord, for giving me the right words when
it really matters.

 When you see an adult becoming hostile to a child, pray immediately for the situation. And if you know the adult, offer her or him a peaceful alternative.

STRENGTH, HOPE, AND PERSPECTIVE

Whatever you have learned or received or heard from me, or seen in me—put it into practice. And the God of peace will be with you. —PHILIPPIANS 4:9 (NIV)

I ATTENDED A FUNERAL FOR A FRIEND WHO DIED OF OVARIAN CANCER. SHE was diagnosed a year after I was with the same cancer. I was stage IV; she was stage III. Yet she died, and I am living.

As my husband, Lynn, and I left the church, I felt angry about the unfairness of it all...until I saw our car and stopped in disbelief. The passenger side was badly dented with paint scraped off. Someone had hit it while we were inside the church but left no note of identification or apology. That elevated my anger.

We headed to a body shop where an employee estimated the cost of the repair and advised us to call our insurance company, verify our deductible, file a hit-and-run accident report, schedule the repair, and make arrangements for a rental car while ours would be at the body shop. "It's unfair," I fumed. "We have to pay for someone else's actions."

Lynn said nothing, which helped me to hear an internal whisper—a combination of my mother's voice and the clear promises I know from the Bible: *Life's not fair. Cancer's not fair. Paying for another's mistakes isn't fair. But Someone already did that. He understands your struggles and gives you strength and hope and perspective, especially when life's not fair.* —CAROL KUYKENDALL

Lord, when I don't understand life's realities, I desperately need Your presence and promises.

 Pray for strength and perspective until the issue is resolved.

SEE THE HUMOR TODAY

Our mouth was filled with laughter. 216 —PSALM 126:2 (RSV)

GOD, CAN YOU OPEN THE GROUND AND LET ME DISAPPEAR? AS EMBARRASSING moments go, this was one of my biggest. I'd been angrily waiting for my girlfriend Sheila and had a feeling that it would be a long wait. To give you an idea, Sheila's license plate frame says, "Always late...but worth the wait." As I waited on a street corner, tapping my foot impatiently, I silently rehashed my negative thoughts: I had told her that I only had forty-five minutes for lunch today since I had a meeting at 1:00 PM sharp.

Another friend was able to shrug off Sheila's lateness as just one of her quirks, and so could I...sometimes. *Oh, why can't she be more considerate?* Still, I knew praying for someone else to change was a losing proposition, so instead I prayed, *God, help me be more tolerant!* And when I saw Sheila racing toward me down the street, I felt calmer and shouted, "I'm not mad at you! Stop running!" Which she did. Immediately.

That's when I saw that the woman who stopped running was not my friend but a complete stranger, who was now walking very slowly past me, giving me an odd look along with plenty of space. And several minutes later, there was Sheila, strolling along as if she didn't have a care in the world. She gave a big smile when she saw me. "Aren't you proud of me? I'm only ten minutes late. Why are you laughing?" But I couldn't answer her because I was laughing too hard, thinking of that stranger's face. And since laughter and anger don't mix at all, I thanked God for answering my prayer in such a funny way. —LINDA NEUKRUG

*Lord, help me see the humor today in something
that would ordinarily make me mad.*

 Recall a funny situation or joke that makes you laugh. Preserve that smile.

GOD'S PORTION

They go out to their work, searching for food.... —JOB 24:5 (NKJV)

MY HUSBAND, KEITH, AND I DECIDED TO DRIVE DOWN TO TULIP TOWN AND wander the fields of vibrant color the Skagit Valley is famous for. Enchanted, we ordered about twenty different varieties for our half-barrel planters. I loved deciding between the American Dream and the Peking Red, the Black Diamond and the Purissima, the Monte Carlo and the Gudoshnik.

We planted the bulbs in September, but it was a bad winter. When spring came, I saw only about one-tenth of the tulips we'd planted. Closer inspection revealed squirrels had lived off our bulbs when other food was really scarce. I was upset and complained loudly, angrily, to Keith, but he only said, "The squirrels needed food."

I grumped about that for a while but slowly came to realize that he was right: Providing nourishment should trump surface beauty every time. I came to see the squirrels as survivors and was glad that the tulips had helped them get through the winter.

Lord, help me to understand more quickly that being part of the balance of life means I don't always get to do things my way. —RHODA BLECKER

I praise You, God, for Your enduring presence, even when
I am angry or frustrated with You.

Share with someone how God gave you a new perspective regarding something that made you angry. Sharing it will help you recall how to heal.

EMBRACING JESUS'S COUNTERINTUITIVE WORDS

Pray for them which despitefully use you, and persecute you.
—MATTHEW 5:44 (NRSV)

A FRIEND CONFIDED THAT SHE WAS A VICTIM OF CYBER-BULLYING. THE harassers sent repeated texts, called work and home at all hours, and posted hurtful comments on social media sites. When she described a particularly cruel attack, I was so angry I couldn't sleep. Something needed to be done, but what? I prayed for my friend, but it didn't seem like nearly enough help.

The next morning I got up to find all the windows open and the heat turned on. "Are you crazy?" I asked my husband, Don. "It's supposed to be 104 today! The air conditioner isn't working right, and the last thing we need is more heat!"

"Our geothermal heat pump heats and cools by circulating water through underground pipes," Don reminded me. "With this drought and string of one-hundred-degree-plus days, the water stays too warm. Turning on the heat actually cools the water, so the air conditioner will run properly when I turn it on again."

It didn't make sense, but it worked. For the first time in three weeks, the house stayed pleasant even when the outside temperature hit the century mark.

Jesus's words are counterintuitive too. Pray for your enemies? For people who try to ruin someone's life? It doesn't make sense. But when I started praying for the harassers, anger stopped ruling my thoughts so that I was able to support my friend while the appropriate people dealt with the situation. —PENNEY SCHWAB

> *Lord, forgive me my sins as I forgive those who sin against me or against those I love.*

 Close your eyes and recall the line "Be still and know that I am God" (Psalm 46:10). Be still, calm, peaceful, open to the presence of God.

EVERYTHING NEEDS SEASONING

Let your speech always be with grace, seasoned with salt....
—Colossians 4:6 (NKJV)

It's 5:00 am when the sirens awake me. We're on the last leg of our vacation, staying in a motel in South Bend, Indiana. I peek out the window to see round after round of police cars and ambulances screaming by.

I can't get back to sleep, so I take a walk until my wife, Sharon, awakes at six o'clock. Together we walk down the street to a little restaurant.

The restaurant seems dead; only one waitress is in sight. We order, but it takes twenty minutes for our food to arrive. Forgetting my manners, I shove biscuits into my mouth and force them down with cranberry juice, but the biscuits are doughy. The eggs are slimy, and the bacon is rubbery. Everything needs seasoning!

"This food is awful," I mutter to Sharon, and she nods her agreement. "This is supposed to be a name-brand restaurant. There's no excuse for this kind of service. This is the last time we ever eat at this place."

At last the waitress arrives with our ticket.

"Was everything okay?" she wants to know.

I feel my jaws clench, and my eyes turn to stone. "I've tasted better."

She blushes. "I'm sorry. There was a big accident on the tollway, and my help hasn't arrived, not even the cook. I'm having to do everything myself. I'm so sorry."

My anger turns to compassion. I leave a big tip, and as I exit, I'm thinking, *Everything needs seasoning, especially me.* —Daniel Schantz

> *Lord, forgive me when I put my own feelings ahead*
> *of the needs of others.*

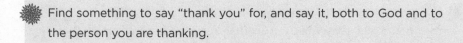 Find something to say "thank you" for, and say it, both to God and to the person you are thanking.

PRAYING AS GOD COMMANDS

"Pray for those who mistreat you." —LUKE 6:28 (NIV)

IT WAS A LOVELY SPRING MORNING AND I WAS ON MY FAVORITE PART OF MY morning prayer walk—the "Thy kingdom come" section when I pray for blessings and provision for the people I know who do ministry of all sorts. *And, Lord, please bless Monty,* I prayed silently. And then it happened for the hundredth time: I replayed an unfortunate incident that had taken place months ago on a mission project. Someone else working with us had been extremely critical of Monty's rules and his ways of doing things. The criticism had undermined Monty's authority and dampened the spiritual atmosphere of the team.

When I prayed for Monty, I found myself becoming upset all over again. I stopped on the sidewalk and thought, *Praying for Monty always drags me down because of how disappointed I am with the fellow who undermined him. Maybe I should stop praying for him since it seems to stir up my bad attitude and makes me think about all of the shortcomings of the guy who criticized him.*

A cloud scooted over the sun and I suddenly realized that I should never give up my prayer walk. Why should I give up on praying for someone because it wasn't easy? I humbly prayed, *Father, I thank You for the difficult prayer.*

Jesus tells us to pray for our enemies. But praying for those I dislike isn't easy; it involves honestly dredging up feelings of disappointment, hurt, anger, and indignation. I continue to pray for Monty daily—only now, I also pray for the fellow who criticized him. It certainly keeps me praying—very hard! —KAREN BARBER

Dear Father, I'd rather not, but You have commanded me to
pray for everyone, even _____.

 Do you have someone you view as an "enemy"? Anonymously submit their name on a prayer list. Follow that up with your own prayer that.

BEAUTY FOR ASHES

To give unto them beauty for ashes... —Isaiah 61:3 (KJV)

My engagement had ended suddenly, and I felt as though I was on the verge of a nervous breakdown. I had to get out of town.

My sister Keri had found a trip leaving for the Bahamas later that day. Before I knew it, I was on Grand Bahama Island, parked on a beach chair, looking out at the emerald-green ocean. I stared for hours, not moving, as the waves rolled back and forth. And then came the crying.

After my second day, I started taking walks down the beach, thinking about why this had happened. My faith was one of the things that had come between my fiancée and me; she was unable to respect my belief in God. I thought I could save her, show her the hope and happiness that faith can bring. In my mind, the stage was being set for God to show up. But to her, He never did.

As I got a good distance down the beach, I began to talk to God. "How could You let this happen to us? This was all about You, after all!" I was sobbing now, stumbling; the sun streaming red and pink lights throughout the stark blue sky. As the ocean continued its ebb and flow, the tide seemed to roar, *Why?*

I was screaming now. "I'm dead inside, God! There's nothing left! If You're there, how can You get me through this pain? What can You possibly give me?"

Suddenly, everything stopped: the sound of the ocean, the wind, my anger. Into my mind, clear and instantly focused, came one word: *you.* —Brock Kidd

Lord, You have redeemed me and claimed me and
given me a strength that is not my own.

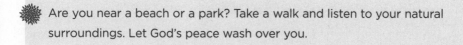
Are you near a beach or a park? Take a walk and listen to your natural surroundings. Let God's peace wash over you.

DON'T WORRY ABOUT TOMORROW

Trust in the Lord with all your heart, and do not rely on your own insight. In all your ways acknowledge him and he will make straight your paths.
—PROVERBS 3:5–6 (NRSV)

MY HUSBAND, CHARLIE, AND I SELDOM FIGHT, BUT WHEN WE DO, IT'S usually devastating for both of us. We're just not very good at it. We usually end up drained and much more distressed about hurting each other than we were about the original problem.

A few months ago we were anxious about what appeared to be a looming crisis. My style in a situation like that is to plan obsessively for all contingencies so that we'll be ready for whatever disaster I imagine will strike. Charlie's way is to wait and see what happens, confident that he will be able to handle whatever occurs.

On this particular occasion we clashed big-time. When, after an exhaustive review of the possibilities, I told him what I planned to do, he looked at me wearily and said, "You're not doing that."

Everything came to a screeching halt. The ensuing crisis had nothing to do with the one we'd been discussing. My determination to *"worry about tomorrow"* despite Jesus's warning (Matthew 6:34) ended up ruining an entire night, causing us both heartache and grief.

Oh, and that looming crisis? It never happened. —MARCI ALBORGHETTI

Father, forgive me for worrying. Please let the painful lessons that You teach me lead me to peace in You.

Don't get angry about things that haven't occurred. Instead, allow someone to speak truth into your worries.

TREAD LIGHTLY

Steer clear of foolish discussions that lead people into the sin of anger with each other. —2 TIMOTHY 2:16 (TLB)

HERE IN FLORIDA, ON THE GULF COAST, WE'RE VERY CAREFUL OF stingrays—those beautiful, gentle creatures who bury themselves in the warm sand next to the shore during mating season. If you step on one accidentally, it'll whip its long tail and jab you with the barb located halfway down it with such velocity that the pain is nearly unbearable.

The county even posts signs along the beaches to warn people to do the "stingray shuffle" in which you keep both feet flat in the sand and shuffle them forward when you enter the ocean. The stingrays won't hurt you as long as you don't step on them. If you tread lightly and shuffle your feet in the sand, they can feel the vibrations and scatter before you come near.

Over the years I've had to learn to do a bit of shuffling, zip my lip, and tread lightly with my friend Brenda when it comes to a few topics of discussion. Our religious and political convictions are light-years apart, and rather than ruin a wonderful friendship when those subjects come up, I do the "stingray shuffle" until I can change the subject. It isn't always easy, since I enjoy a good discussion, but I also know that neither of us is willing to stray from our convictions.

Brenda's willingness to do the shuffle, too, has maintained our close friendship to the point that she was my official witness when Jack and I married in 2012.

She's a keeper! —PATRICIA LORENZ

Heavenly Father, You are the Master Negotiator. Help me to tread lightly when it comes to words that can cause pain or disagreement.

 Do you know a loved one's trigger? Do they know yours? Practice the "stingray shuffle" and see what happens.

GO WITH THE EMOTIONAL FLOW

How precious to me are thy thoughts, O God! How vast is the sum of them!
—PSALM 139:17 (RSV)

"I'M *BAD*! I'M THE WORST PERSON IN THE WORLD!"

It's bedtime, and I've been sitting with eleven-year-old John, trying to help him deal with his latest ant attack. Whenever John is punished—or just admonished—for doing something wrong, the litany begins. In his mind every infraction is a major offense and every setback is an unredeemable disaster. His therapist calls them "ants"—*a*utomatic *n*egative *t*houghts. Julia and I are trying to help John set out ant traps to short-circuit his negative thinking. Usually that means trying to help him sort out his feelings and deal with some of the underlying fears that bring on his ants.

In working with John, I've come to recognize ants in my own thoughts. Ironically enough for someone who works in an organization based on positive thinking, my first reaction to setbacks is often to assume the worst: If I'm having trouble with a work project, then I'm just showing that I'm untalented. If Julia is irritated by something I've done, then our marriage is in danger. Neither of these things is true, but I have to step back and look at them rationally to know this. If I don't, I'm opening the door to anger and depression.

I try telling John about my ants. After fifteen minutes of talking, both our ants have fallen into the trap and John is feeling better. "Thanks for telling me, Dad," John says. "Can we say evening prayers?"

I get my prayer book and the Bible. We share some Scriptures and prayers. Then I put my arm around him and walk him to bed. —ANDREW ATTAWAY

Lord, Your Word is the best ant trap of all.

 Breathe in "God created me" and exhale "God loves me".

Lord, sometimes I am all too quick to speak and all too quick to become angry. Forgive me for these sins. I don't want to be this way. Please, God, put a guard over my mouth today. When angry, bitter, unkind, or impatient words bubble up inside me, help me to keep quiet and lay them before You in repentance. May the words from my mouth be pleasing to You today and always. Be glorified in my speech. Let my words be a welcome, sweet offering.

KATIE GANSHERT

Index

A Note from the Editors

We hope you enjoyed *Holding God's Hand*, published by the Books and Inspirational Media Division of Guideposts, a nonprofit organization that touches millions of lives every day through products and services that inspire, encourage, help you grow in your faith, and celebrate God's love.

Thank you for making a difference with your purchase of this book, which helps fund our many outreach programs to military personnel, prisons, hospitals, nursing homes, and educational institutions.

We also create many useful and uplifting online resources. Visit Guideposts.org to read true stories of hope and inspiration, access OurPrayer network, sign up for free newsletters, download free e-books, join our Facebook community, and follow our stimulating blogs.

To learn about other Guideposts publications, including the best-selling devotional *Daily Guideposts*, go to Guideposts.org/Shop, call (800) 932-2145, or write to Guideposts, PO Box 5815, Harlan, Iowa 51593.

Discover resources that help connect faith-filled values to your daily life

Digging Deeper

Enrich your devotional time with additional Scripture readings referenced at the close of each day's devotion.

 DailyGuideposts.org

Free Newsletters

Sign up for newsletters on positive living, faith in daily life, helping others, the power of prayer, and more!

 Guideposts.org/Newsletters

Free eBooks

Visit us to download more inspirational reading on subjects like prayer, personal growth, and positive thinking.

 Guideposts.org/SpiritLifters

Follow Us on Social Media

See what's happening with your favorite authors and more!

 DailyGuideposts

 DailyGuideposts

DAILY GUIDEPOSTS

Celebrating 40 years of spirit-lifting devotions